ON THE TRAIL *of the* MORTIMERS
in the WELSH MARCHES

First published by Logaston Press in 2016. Reprinted in 2017, 2018.
This revised and extended edition published October 2022, reprinted March 2024
by Logaston Press, The Holme, Church Road, Eardisley, Herefordshire HR3 6NJ.
logastonpress.co.uk

Text Copyright © Philip Hume 2016 and 2022.
Photographs Copyright © Philip Hume 2016 and 2022, except where otherwise acknowledged.

All rights reserved.
The moral right of the author has been asserted.

Without limiting the rights under copyright reserved above, no part of this publication may be reproduced, stored in or introduced into a retrieval system, or transmitted, in any form or by any means (electronic, mechanical, photocopying, recording or otherwise), without prior written permission of the copyright owner and the above publisher of this book.

ISBN 978-1-910839-59-1

Designed and typeset by Richard Wheeler in 10.5 on 14.5 Caslon.
Cover design by Logaston Press.

Printed and bound in Poland www.lfbookservices.co.uk

Logaston Press is committed to a sustainable future for our business,
our readers and our planet. The book in your hand is made from FSC® certified paper

British Library Catalogue in Publishing data.
A CIP catalogue record for this book is available from the British Library.

ON THE TRAIL *of the* MORTIMERS
in the WELSH MARCHES

*Earls of March, Lords of Wigmore and Ludlow –
the story of a dynasty and the places that
give an insight into their lives*

Philip Hume

LOGASTON PRESS

Ludlow castle

This book is dedicated to John Grove, who had the vision to set up the Mortimer History Society, the inspiration for this tour, and who has been an invaluable historical consultant.

In the first edition I expressed my gratitude to friends and colleagues across the locations, who had been happy to share their enthusiasm and knowledge of local history and the Mortimers. Six years on, and having had the pleasure to meet many more people (some, indeed, who had been inspired by the book to visit the locations), I continue to be grateful. Particular thanks go to Bob Anderson, Paul R. Davis, Julian Ravest and Chris Jones-Jenkins for their kind permission to use their excellent images. Andy Johnson provided the design and layout of the first edition, which first attracted many people to pick it up from the bookshelves. My thanks also now to Su & Richard Wheeler who have refreshed the design of this revised and enhanced edition.

Philip Hume, June 2022

The Mortimer History Society

The Mortimer History Society promotes the study and dissemination of information about both the Mortimer family of Wigmore and the medieval Marcher lordships. The Society's conferences and events, journals, annual Essay Prize, newsletters, and website are a mine of information: mortimerhistorysociety.org.uk

The third in a series of publications for the MHS

CONTENTS

NOTE ON USE OF NAMES	*vi*
HOW TO USE THIS BOOK AND TOUR	*vii*
SELECT FAMILY TREE OF THE MORTIMERS	*viii*
INTRODUCTION	*ix*
MORTIMER TIMELINE	*xi*
INNER MORTIMER TOUR MAP	*xiv*
OUTER MORTIMER TOUR MAP	*xvii*
GENEALOGY OF NORMAN AND PLANTAGENET KINGS	*xviii*
ONE: Conquest in England and Wales: 1066–1214	1
TWO: Consolidation and Expansion: 1214–1304	21
THREE: King in Name or King of Folly: 1304–30	37
FOUR: Recovery and a Claim to the Throne: 1330–1425	53
FIVE: A Mortimer Descendant Wins the Throne in Battle: 1425–80	67
Postscript: Ludlow, Capital of the Marches	77
Inner Mortimer Tour	79
Outer Mortimer Tour	129
OTHER MORTIMER PLACES TO VISIT	151
FURTHER READING	157

NOTE ON USE OF NAMES

The Mortimers often named their eldest son after the child's grandfather, and thus there are six Roger Mortimers over the course of 13 generations, and four Edmunds. To ensure clarity about which Mortimer is being referred to, the first time a name is used, and subsequently depending on context, it is followed in brackets by the date of death. These cross-refer to the dates in the family tree. Also in the interests of clarity, whilst the French style of naming is used for the first Norman lord who probably never came to England (with the use of 'de'), thereafter the English version is used.

CONTENTS

NOTE ON USE OF NAMES	*vi*
HOW TO USE THIS BOOK AND TOUR	*vii*
SELECT FAMILY TREE OF THE MORTIMERS	*viii*
INTRODUCTION	*ix*
MORTIMER TIMELINE	*xi*
INNER MORTIMER TOUR MAP	*xiv*
OUTER MORTIMER TOUR MAP	*xvii*
GENEALOGY OF NORMAN AND PLANTAGENET KINGS	*xviii*
ONE: Conquest in England and Wales: 1066–1214	1
TWO: Consolidation and Expansion: 1214–1304	21
THREE: King in Name or King of Folly: 1304–30	37
FOUR: Recovery and a Claim to the Throne: 1330–1425	53
FIVE: A Mortimer Descendant Wins the Throne in Battle: 1425–80	67
Postscript: Ludlow, Capital of the Marches	77
Inner Mortimer Tour	79
Outer Mortimer Tour	129
OTHER MORTIMER PLACES TO VISIT	151
FURTHER READING	157

NOTE ON USE OF NAMES

The Mortimers often named their eldest son after the child's grandfather, and thus there are six Roger Mortimers over the course of 13 generations, and four Edmunds. To ensure clarity about which Mortimer is being referred to, the first time a name is used, and subsequently depending on context, it is followed in brackets by the date of death. These cross-refer to the dates in the family tree. Also in the interests of clarity, whilst the French style of naming is used for the first Norman lord who probably never came to England (with the use of 'de'), thereafter the English version is used.

HOW TO USE THIS BOOK AND TOUR

This book interweaves the history of the Mortimer family with those locations, buildings and artefacts on the tour that provide a touchstone and connection to their history, with insights into life across the period.

The first part of the book provides a brief history of the Mortimer family; the second part gives details of what can be seen on the suggested tour. The inner tour focusses on the core area of Mortimer power centred around Wigmore and Ludlow; the outer tour reflects the growth of the Mortimers' influence as they rose to dominate the Welsh Marches. The third part lists sites further afield connected to the Mortimers that can easily be visited.

The maps on pages *xiv–xv* and *xvii* show the route of the tour. The tour is arranged simply as a guide to get from one location to another: it does not follow any chronological or other historical order, and you will almost certainly need a proper OS or road map to find some of the villages. You can start and finish wherever you choose, or simply visit those locations which are of greatest interest to you.

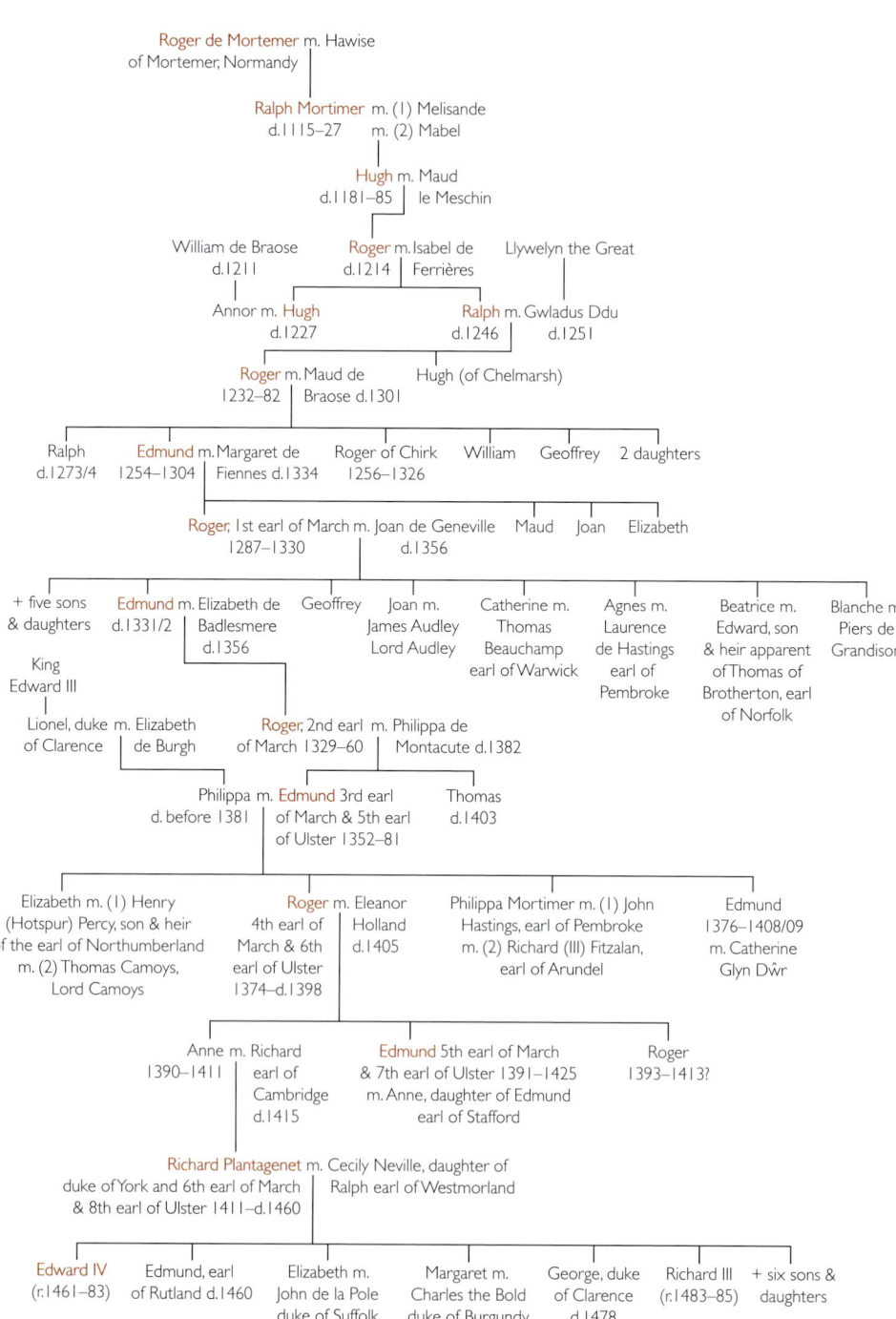

Select family tree of the Mortimers

INTRODUCTION

Most visitors to, and residents of, the area bordering north Herefordshire, south Shropshire and Wales are aware of the name 'Mortimer' which has been used to designate not only a wide area as 'Mortimer Country', but also to name a forest, a road junction, a food store, a walking trail, a restaurant, a cider and much else. Far fewer, though, are aware of who the Mortimers were, their vivid history and why the connection to this area is so important. This was the motivation to write the first edition which focussed on the 'inner tour' of this book.

People now live in and visit the area for its quiet, natural rural beauty, enchanting countryside and remoteness. Yet for 500 turbulent years following the Conquest in 1066 this area was the centre of dramatic and important events: ruled over by powerful lords, it was the site of battles that affected the destiny of the country and was regularly visited by kings and queens. Indeed, the important role that the people and this area had in the country's history is reflected in such well-known London places as Mortimer Street, Wigmore Street, the Wigmore Hall and Harley Street.

Also, when asked to define the Welsh Marches, many would describe it as the border region of Herefordshire, Shropshire and Powys. Yet, throughout the medieval period, the Welsh Marches encompassed an area that ran from the north-east coast of Wales, down to the Severn Estuary, and across all of south Wales to the west coast of Pembrokeshire. The territory was defined by the 50 or so powerful, independent Marcher lordships that formed a region between the lands of England and the Principality of Wales. From their base at Wigmore, the Mortimer family grew to dominate the Welsh Marches, controlling a third of the Marcher lordships. Hence, it became logical to extend the scope of this edition to include an 'outer tour' of Mortimer locations across the Marches.

The tour and the book use the physical remains from that period to give an insight into how the Mortimer family came from Normandy, became established in Wigmore and the surrounding area and, over the centuries, rose to be one of the most powerful families in the land. Partly through the good fortune of having an unbroken male succession for over 350 years, and also through conquest, marriage and royal favour, they amassed a great empire of estates in England, Wales and Ireland; played key roles in the changing balance of power between the monarchy and nobles; deposed a king and virtually ruled the kingdom for three years; became, in later generations, close heirs to the throne through marriage; and seized the throne through battle when a Mortimer grandson became King Edward IV.

Following the Conquest, the Normans stamped their authority on the country through the power of their castles as visible and practical statements of their military control; subsequent generations spent their wealth to improve the defences and to develop the castles as more comfortable and palatial places to live. They demonstrated their piety through support for churches, which were built in stone so also dominated the countryside.

Indeed, the borderlands between England and Wales had some of the highest concentrations of castles anywhere in medieval Europe – within the small area of the inner tour alone there are the ruins and visible sites of no fewer than 17 castles (and there were more), 15 churches, an abbey and a priory, which all have links to the Mortimer family and which are visible reminders of their lordship and domination of the area. There are also three sites of battles, conflict and routs which affected the course of national events. Nowadays, some of the castles appear as romantic ruins, whilst others are sites where you have to use your imagination to summon up the past; most of the churches are still regularly used for worship.

MORTIMER TIMELINE

KEY NATIONAL EVENTS	DATES	KEY MORTIMER EVENTS
	1054	Duke William takes Mortemer Castle off Roger (d.1078–84)
Norman Conquest of England. Duke William becomes King William I	1066	
	1075	Ralph (d.1115–27) given Wigmore, Orleton, Shobdon, Leintwardine, Aston, Pilleth
Domesday Book	1086	
William 'Rufus' II becomes king	1087	
	c.1090s	Mortimers take Maelienydd for the first time
Henry I becomes king	1100	
	c.1120	Hugh (d.1181–85) becomes lord of Wigmore
Stephen becomes king	1135	
'The Anarchy' of Civil War between Stephen and Matilda	1138 –1153	Hugh leads local faction loyal to Stephen He is imprisoned for a while in Ludlow Castle
	1130s –1150s	Herefordshire School of Romanesque Sculpture active – incl. Pipe Aston, Orleton, Shobdon
Henry II becomes king	1154	
		Maelienydd lost back to the Welsh
	1179	Wigmore Abbey is dedicated
	c.1180	Roger (d.1214) becomes lord of Wigmore
Richard I 'The Lionheart' becomes king and leads crusade to recapture Jerusalem	1189	
	1195	Roger regains Maelienydd
John becomes king	1199	
	1207	Roger granted Knighton and it's taken away
	1214	Hugh (d.1227) becomes lord of Wigmore
Magna Carta	1215	Welsh regain Maelienydd and Knighton
Henry III becomes king	1216	
Magna Carta re-issued	1225	
	1227	Ralph (d.1246) becomes lord of Wigmore
	1230	Ralph marries Gwladus Ddu, has custody of Presteigne and regains Knighton
	1240s	Ralph rebuilds Knighton, Cefnllys and Knucklas Castles, and regains Maelienydd
	1246	Roger (d.1282) becomes lord of Wigmore
	1247	Roger marries Maud de Braose and gains Kingsland, Radnor, Narberth and parts of St Clears and Haverford

xi

KEY NATIONAL EVENTS	DATES	KEY MORTIMER EVENTS
	1260 –1262	Presteigne, Knighton, Cefnllys and Knucklas castles captured and sacked by Llywelyn ap Gruffudd, and Maelienydd lost
	1264	Wigmore Castle captured by Simon de Montfort
Battle of Evesham – death of Simon de Montfort	1265	Simon de Montfort's head delivered to Wigmore Pembridge Castle forced from de Pembridge family
Edward I becomes king whilst on crusade	1272	Roger (d.1282) virtual regent while new king abroad
First Edwardian conquest of Wales	1277	Roger leads one of the armies, capturing Dolforwyn Castle, and regaining Maelienydd
	1279	Roger rewarded with lordships of Ceri and Cedewain
Final Edwardian conquest of Wales	1282	Edmund (d.1304) becomes lord of Wigmore, and his brother, Roger, granted Chirk
	1301	Roger (d.1330) marries Joan de Geneville, heiress of Ludlow, at Pembridge, and gains a share of Ewyas Lacy
	1304	Roger becomes lord of Wigmore
Edward II becomes King	1307	
Battle of Bannockburn	1314	Roger fights in rearguard and is captured
	1322	Roger rebels, is captured and imprisoned in the Tower of London
	1323	Roger escapes from the Tower and flees to France
	1325	Queen Isabella leads diplomatic mission to France and is later joined by her son, Prince Edward
	1326	Roger and Queen Isabella return with small army and gain support
Edward II deposed and disappears; Edward III becomes king	1327 –1330	Roger and Isabella rule the country as new king is a minor, but Roger does not take formal role on council, and was granted Denbigh, Montgomery, Builth and Clifford
	1328	Roger raised to rank of earl of March
	1330	Roger captured, executed for treason, and land and titles confiscated. Edmund (d.1331/2) becomes lord of Wigmore
	1331	Roger (d.1360), aged 3, becomes lord of Wigmore
Battle of Crécy	1346	Roger fights well at Crécy
	1348	Roger is one of the founding members of the Order of the Garter
	1353	King Edward III twice visits St Mary Magdalene, Leintwardine

KEY NATIONAL EVENTS	DATES	KEY MORTIMER EVENTS
	1354	Judgement on Roger (d.1330) annulled and title of earl of March with all estates restored
	1360	Edmund (d.1381), aged 8, becomes 3rd earl of March
	1368	Edmund marries Philippa, daughter of Lionel of Antwerp, gaining Usk
Richard II becomes king	1377	
	1381	Roger (d.1398), aged 7, becomes 4th earl of March
	1398	Edmund (d.1425), aged 7, becomes 5th earl of March
Richard II deposed and murdered; Henry IV becomes king	1399	Edmund and his brother taken under royal control
Welsh rebellion of Glyn Dŵr	1402	Battle of Pilleth, Sir Edmund Mortimer defeated
Henry V becomes king	1413	
Battle of Agincourt	1415	Plot to depose Henry V and replace him with Edmund fails
Henry VI becomes king	1422	
	1425	Edmund dies and the Mortimer inheritance passes to his sister's son, Richard, duke of York
	1452	Edward (future king) and his brother live at Ludlow
Richard, duke of York becomes Protector	1453	
Battle of St Albans	1455	
Rout of Ludford Bridge	1459	Ludlow ransacked
Richard, duke of York killed at Battle of Wakefield	1460	
Battle of Mortimer's Cross and Edward IV proclaimed king and crowned after battle of Towton	1461	Edward IV spends a week in Ludlow
	1473	Prince Edward, aged 3, lives at Ludlow with the 'Prince's Council'
King Edward IV dies; coronation of Prince Edward does not happen; Richard III becomes king	1483	Prince Edward leaves Ludlow to travel to London but is taken into custody of his uncle and disappears
Richard III killed at Bosworth; Henry (Tudor) VII becomes king and marries Elizabeth, daughter of Edward IV	1485	
Prince Arthur dies at Ludlow Castle	1502	Prince Arthur's heart interred in St Laurence's, Ludlow
Henry VIII becomes king	1509	
	1525–1528	Princess Mary lives at Ludlow Castle for 3 winters
Council of the Marches abolished	1689	

xiii

INNER MORTIMER TOUR MAP

(See pp. 79-128 for details of the Inner Tour)

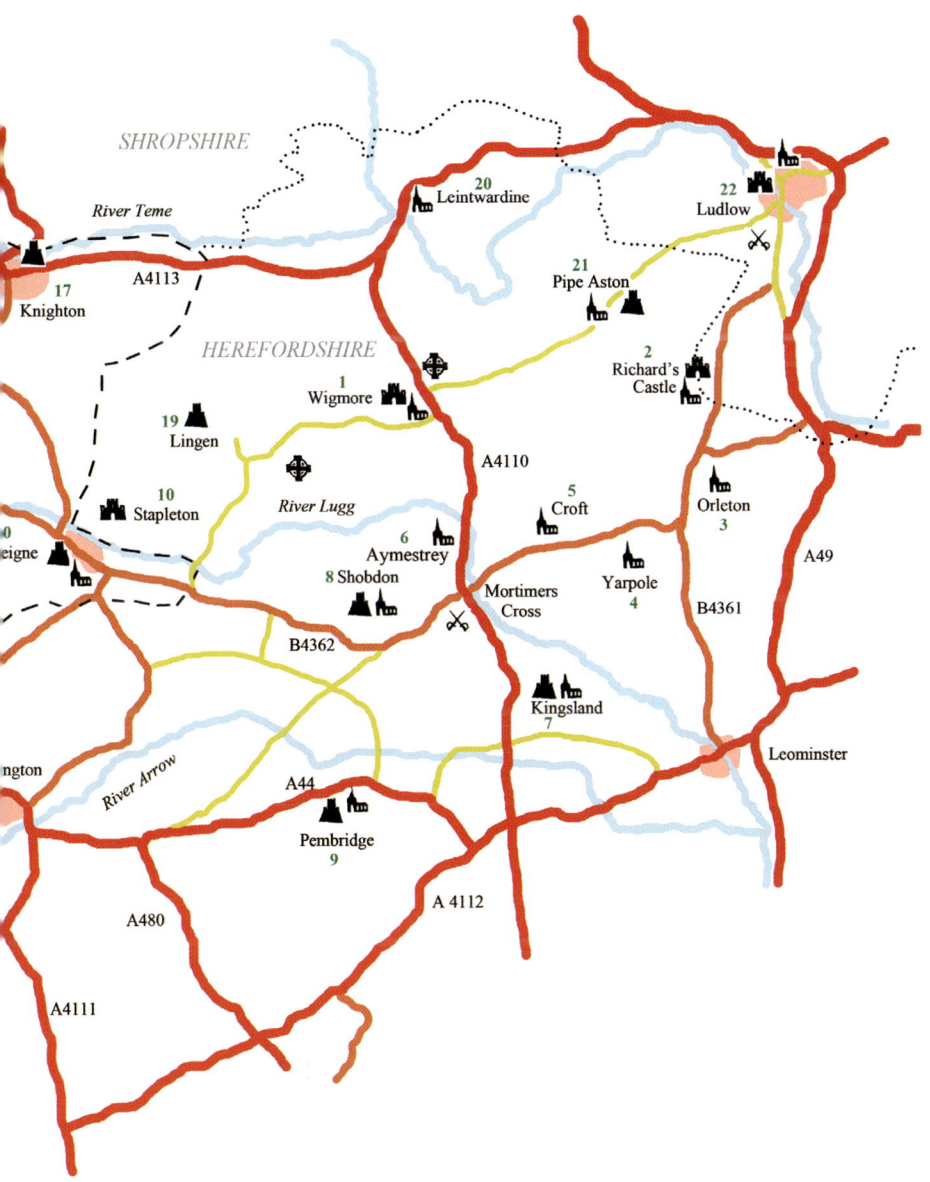

A view of Longtown Castle in 1840, by Charles Walter Radclyffe, published in *Picturesque Antiquities &c. of the County of Hereford*

OUTER MORTIMER TOUR MAP

(See pp. 129-150 for details of the Outer Tour)

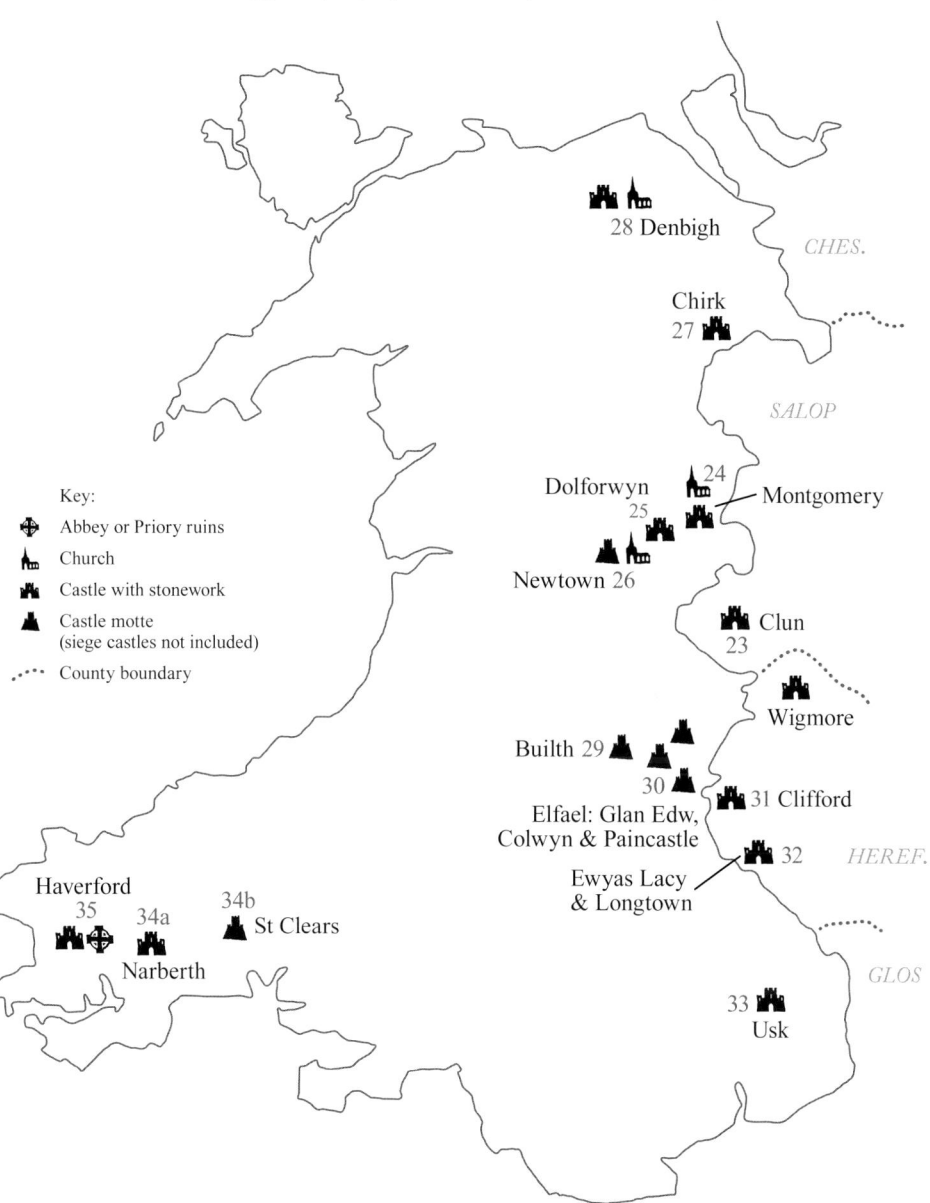

SIMPLIFIED GENEALOGY OF THE NORMAN AND PLANTAGENET KINGS

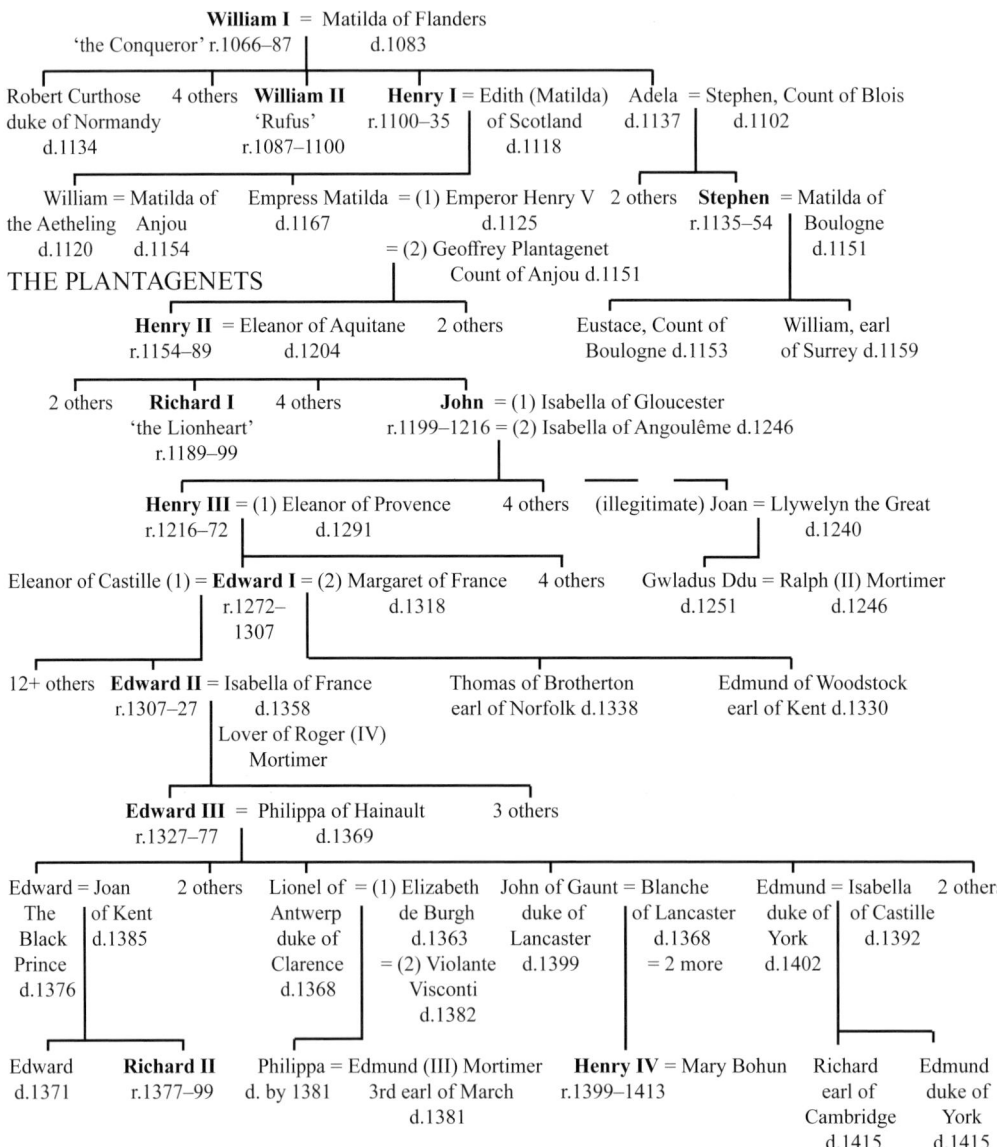

ONE

Conquest in England and Wales: 1066–1214

This section recounts where the Mortimer name came from; how the family were established as lords of Wigmore after the Norman Conquest and sought, by warfare, to conquer more lands in Wales. Nationally, the Mortimers were in the second rank of barons and were not particularly significant in national affairs, but by the end of this period they were well-placed to use skills in war, royal service and advantageous marriages to gain more land, power and prestige in the following century. This period covers the first four generations of Mortimers: Roger (d.1078–84); Ralph (d.1115–27); Hugh (d.1181–85); Roger (d.1214).

Written documentation and evidence from this period is scarce so it is not possible to see much more than outlines and particular points in the lives of the Mortimer lords. In most cases the dates of their births and deaths are not recorded and can only be deduced from when they are first mentioned in those records that do exist and when they cease to be mentioned. Indeed, historians have disputed (see later in this section) over the descent of the Mortimers, with some wrongly including an extra generation in the genealogy.

Although the written evidence is scarce, the area covered by the tours contains many physical remains that testify to the arrival of the Mortimers, their increasing power over land and people, the turmoil of war with the native kingdoms of Wales, and also of anarchy and civil war in England when the throne was disputed for nearly 20 years between 1135 and 1154.

The first person to use the name Mortimer was Roger de Mortemer (d.1078–84), a distant relative of Duke William of Normandy (later King William I, the Conqueror, of England). When Roger was still a young man, the duke gave him custody of the castle of Mortemer-sur-Eaulne on the frontier between the

> **THE WIGMORE CHRONICLE**
>
> The Wigmore Chronicle, an important source of information about the early history of the Mortimers, in fact comprises four separate texts. The first, written in the 1390s and incorporating a chronicle written over a century earlier in about 1262, was compiled to demonstrate the Mortimer claim to the throne. The second text, which is incorporated in the same document as the first, is an account of the foundation of Wigmore Abbey. The third is an annual list of events covering the period 1105–1306, and the fourth contains extracts from a chronicle that describes the years 1360–77. In many of their details, but not all, the texts are supported by other sources.

lands of the duchy of Normandy and those of the King of France. In 1054, when the King of France invaded Normandy, Roger de Mortimer was the joint leader with Robert, Count of Eu, of a force that defeated the king in a battle near Mortemer – he probably took his name from the battle in which he was the victor, rather than the castle of Mortemer, which he held only a short time.

During the battle, Roger took captive Ralph de Montdidier, Count of Amiens and, later, of Valois, an important ally of the king and enemy of Duke William. However, the count was also Roger's overlord for some of his lands and so was released by Roger. At first Duke William was furious and banished Roger, confiscating all his estates in Normandy. When they were reconciled, the duke restored everything to Roger except Mortemer, which he and the family never owned again.

It is unclear whether a de Mortemer fought at Hastings in 1066 when Duke William began his campaign to take the English Crown. One account refers to a Hugh de Mortemer leading a charge, but Roger is the only known male of the family in the right age bracket who could have taken part in the battle. So, whether it is a confusion over the names or a story that was made up to link the family to the 'glory' of the Conquest, it is impossible to say.

What is certain is that Roger's son, Ralph Mortimer (d.1115–27) came over to England and was given extensive lands as well as inheriting the family estates in Normandy. His date of birth in Normandy is not known and the first recorded references to Ralph relate to the lands that he acquired in England after 1075.

William the Conqueror created three large earldoms: Chester, Shrewsbury

Wigmore Castle controlled the strategic routes across the glacial plain

Aerial view of Wigmore Castle (© Paul R. Davis)

and Hereford, to control the Welsh border. The earls of Hereford had started to build Wigmore Castle but when the 2nd earl rebelled in 1075 all his lands were taken from him and Wigmore was given to Ralph, who made it his chief residence and central lordship of the Mortimer estates. It may well be that Ralph was being rewarded for his role in suppressing the rebellion of a local colourful Saxon magnate, Edric the Wild. Wigmore Castle remained the principal residence of the Mortimers for over 250 years until it was gradually superseded by Ludlow Castle which they acquired by marriage in 1301.

In 1075 or soon after Ralph was also given several manors that had belonged, up to her death that year, to Queen Edith, the widow of Edward the Confessor, King of England between 1042 and 1066, including Orleton and Shobdon on the inner tour. In 1086, William I compiled Domesday Book to record who owned all land and property (and thus owed taxes) in the country. From Domesday, it is known that by 1086 Ralph owned more than 100 manors in 12 counties spread across England – Yorkshire, Lincolnshire, Warwickshire, Leicestershire, Herefordshire, Shropshire, Worcestershire, Oxfordshire, Wiltshire, Berkshire, Somerset and Hampshire.

In addition to Wigmore, Orleton and Shobdon on the inner tour, Ralph Mortimer is recorded in Domesday as owning Leintwardine, Leinthall Earls and Starkes, Pipe Aston and one outlying estate within the manor of Kingsland. Pilleth in Wales, where there is a site of a motte and bailey castle which may have been erected by Ralph Mortimer some time after 1086, was a western outlier of the Wigmore lordship. The other locations on the inner and outer tours came into Mortimer ownership through conquest, force and advantageous marriages over the next 250 years.

Nationally, Ralph was not especially prominent during the time of William I. When he died in 1087, William split his inheritance so that his eldest son, Robert, inherited Normandy, the second son, William Rufus, England, and the third son, Henry received money. Inevitably, this led to tension and difficulties, particularly as most of the barons owned estates on both sides of the Channel. Ralph was with Duke Robert in Normandy in early 1088 when they may have discussed the possibility of an invasion of England. In the summer of 1088, Ralph and other Marcher barons, including Richard fitz Scrob (see box opposite), were involved in rebellion against William Rufus but were defeated at Worcester. It appears, though, that Ralph was soon forgiven. On the death of Rufus, Henry, the Conqueror's youngest son, became king and Ralph is recorded as siding with him against Duke Robert in 1104.

THE MORTIMERS OF RICHARDS CASTLE

At this point in the history of the Mortimers it is appropriate to take a quick detour both on the tour and in the story. The road between Ludlow and Orleton goes through Richards Castle where the castle is well worth visiting. Predating the Norman Conquest, it is one of the oldest castle sites in England, and was held for a while by a separate family of Mortimers. Next to the castle, the church is one of three on this tour that has a separate bell tower (there are fewer than 50 in the whole of England).

King Edward the Confessor (r.1042–66) had been raised in exile in the Norman Court. When he succeeded to the English throne he brought Norman ways and customs with him – and Norman friends to whom he gave grants of land, including along the Welsh border. To counter raids from Wales, Edward also gave permission to build castles in the border region. One to benefit was Richard fitz Scrob, given land at Auretone (now Overton) in c.1050, where he built what became known as Richards Castle. The local people were unhappy at this foreign innovation: fortifying a town was one thing; building a private castle to lord it over the neighbours was another. It was, though, a foretaste of the eruption of castle-building after 1066.

During the civil wars of 1138–54 the descendants of fitz Scrob were close allies of Hugh Mortimer (d.1181–85) and for a period the strongholds of Wigmore and Richards Castle were the only ones in north Herefordshire and south Shropshire loyal to King Stephen.

Through marriage, in 1210 Richards Castle came into the possession of Robert Mortimer, who came from a family of Mortimers from Essex. There has been no evidence of a family relationship between the two Mortimer families of Wigmore and Richards Castle; however, recent research by Dr Ian Mortimer has discovered that such a relationship, though distant, does exist. Robert and his descendants owned Richards Castle for the next nearly 100 years until 1304, and as part of the lordship were also owners of Yarpole, and of Stapleton Castle outside Presteigne.

CONQUEST IN ENGLAND AND WALES: 1066–1214

The Norman Marcher lords (see insert box on pp. 18–20) along the Welsh borders had from their inception waged war into Wales to take control of more territory, and the Mortimers were no exception. At some point, possibly in the 1090s, Ralph acquired through conquest Maelienydd, part of the independent region of Rhwng Gwy a Hafren (the Lands between the Wye and the Severn), which adjoined the Mortimer lands in Herefordshire and Shropshire, building a castle at Cymaron. The Mortimers also acquired the independent lands of Gwerthrynion which lay on the western border of Maelienydd (see map on p. 20). The Mortimers were to fight the Welsh for the next 200 years with control of Maelienydd and Gwerthrynion passing back and forth until the final collapse of Welsh independence at the end of the thirteenth century.

From 1086, Ralph started to give some pieces of land to Wigmore parish church and in 1100 he endowed it as a college of three prebends. Soon after though he disappears from the records and, indeed, there is no actual clear record of a Mortimer being in England between the years 1100 and 1139 (though his oldest son might have been). It appears that Ralph died in Normandy sometime between 1115 (when there is a reference to his tenure of a manor in Lincolnshire) and 1127 (when there is a reference to his son witnessing a charter).

Ralph was succeeded by Hugh (d.1181–85), who was possibly his second son. There is no record either of Hugh's date of birth or death. Both Ralph and Hugh were long-lived for their period – Ralph will have been in his 60s or 70s when he died (assuming a date of birth in the 1050s and death between 1115–27). Hugh lived at least well into his 80s and possibly into his 90s (he is likely to have been born in the early 1090s; there is a record that Hugh's eldest son was responsible for his debts in 1181, whilst the Wigmore Chronicle records his death as 1185). Indeed, this was so unusual that some twentieth-century genealogies inserted an additional generation, in effect attributing Hugh's life to two separate generations of Hugh Mortimer. However, recent work by the historian Dr Ian Mortimer (no relation) has shown that there is strong evidence that Hugh really did live to be that old.

Hugh seems to have grown up in Normandy and travelled to England in the late 1130s, which was a time of anarchy and civil war. King Henry I, who died in 1135 without any living legitimate sons, had required the barons to swear allegiance to his daughter the Empress Matilda. Many were unhappy, however, about the idea of a female monarch, whilst Matilda is known to have had a haughty personality which easily alienated people. Thus, when Henry died and his nephew Stephen claimed the throne, many barons gave him their support.

Ludlow Castle looking south-east (© Paul R. Davis)

Anarchy followed when Matilda contested this with warfare, and a devastating civil war occupied most of Stephen's reign. Much of Herefordshire and south Shropshire were repeatedly laid waste by one side or the other.

Matilda, who had first been married to the emperor of Germany, was now married to Geoffrey of Anjou – hence, her faction were known as the 'Angevins'. Matilda's most prominent supporter and military leader was her half-brother (an illegitimate son of Henry I), Robert, earl of Gloucester. Another supporter was Miles, Sheriff of Gloucester (and later earl of Hereford). The south-west and the Marches were thus the major stronghold in the country for Matilda and the Angevins.

Within Herefordshire, only a small group of lords in the north of the county remained loyal to King Stephen – Hugh Mortimer at Wigmore, Osbern fitz Hugh of Richards Castle, William de Braose of Radnor and Kingsland, and initially Joce de Dinan, who now held Ludlow through his wife, Sybil, a descendant of one of the branches of the de Lacy family who had first built Ludlow Castle. It appears that this group met with King Stephen in late 1139 and early 1140, both times at Little Hereford. An important factor for them in remaining loyal to Stephen was that of all the tenants-in-chief in the county (see box on Feudalism overleaf), these three barons had the majority of their landed wealth in areas that were controlled by the king.

FEUDALISM AND RANKS IN SOCIETY

Following the Norman Conquest the system known as feudalism developed. The basis of feudalism was that the great landholders (both nobles and Church) held their land directly from the king and as such came to be called 'tenants-in-chief'. They had to perform an act of homage to the king during which they placed their hands between his and swore allegiance for the land they held from him. The land was usually called a 'feodum' or fee – hence feudalism. The ceremony was solemn and important. Breach of the oath was treason and involved forfeiture of the fief. In return for the land each lord was required to provide knights for the royal army or to guard royal castles, the numbers depending on the value of the land. The 'tenants-in-chief' developed similar relationships with their own tenants.

As well as military service, the feudal system provided the king with sources of money and patronage. When a tenant-in-chief died his son had to make a payment to inherit the fee, described as a 'relief' when considered a reasonable amount and a 'fine' when arbitrary and exorbitant (a form of inheritance tax). If the heir was under-age the wardship of the lands and the income from them passed to the king. The king also controlled the marriages of widows of tenants-in-chief (restricted later by Magna Carta) and those of heirs and heiresses when they were his wards. The king could give the rights of wardship to other nobles. In the absence of any heirs the 'fee' would return ('escheat') to the king who could give it to one of his favourites. Increasingly, kings exploited the system to raise more and more money, which was one of the causes of the disputes that led to Magna Carta, much of which limited future opportunities for royal abuse.

The ranks, after the king, referred to in this book are:

- **Dukes**   the highest rank, but only created in 1337 for Edward III's eldest son, Prince Edward (later known as the Black Prince) and normally a title only given to members of the royal family.
- **Earls**   the number of earls at any one time fluctuated, but usually there were no more than about 14.
- **Barons**   the lowest rank of the aristocracy with numbers fluctuating either side of 50.

> All these lords were tenants-in-chief holding their lands directly from the king, though barons might also hold land from the earls.
>
> The next tier in the feudal hierarchy comprised the local lords, bannerets (knights who led a company of troops during time of war under their own banner), knights, esquires and gentlemen who held land from the dukes, earls and barons.

Hugh Mortimer assumed leadership of this royalist faction. An indication of how intense and precarious their position was in the central Marches can be seen from the fact that none of them is ever recorded to be in the king's company from this time to the end of the civil war in 1153, suggesting that their presence was required in the Marches in order to retain their lands.

One aspect of the Anarchy was the confusion caused as lords switched sides, made worse by some using it as an excuse to pursue bloody personal feuds. Some of the locations on the tour give an insight into the disputes and violence of this period as recounted below. Despite this, however, there were still opportunities and times of peace to build churches, spurred on no doubt by the increased prospect of sudden death in the outbreaks of violence.

Hugh Mortimer had rewarded the family's loyal steward, Oliver de Merlimond, by giving him the manor of Shobdon. Oliver immediately began to build a stone church between 1136 and 1141, which played an important role in the development of the Herefordshire School of Romanesque Sculpture (see insert on p. 12). Whilst the church was being built, Oliver undertook a pilgrimage to St James of Santiago de Compostela in Spain, staying in Paris on the way. On his return he established a priory at Shobdon and gave churches and lands in his gift to fund two canons who were sent from Paris to live in a house near the church – after three subsequent moves to different sites this foundation eventually became Wigmore Abbey.

The Anarchy soon intervened in 1143 when Oliver de Merlimond broke with Hugh Mortimer and transferred his allegiance to Miles, earl of Hereford causing a 'very great and violent quarrel between him and Hugh'. Oliver may have done this because he felt that the royalist cause led by Hugh was hopeless. He may also have felt that the, locally much larger, Angevin faction were in a better position to commission work from the sculptors who had now completed the church at Shobdon. Hugh stripped Oliver of all his possessions and initially vented his rage on the canons at Shobdon, seeking to drive them out, before relenting and allowing them to stay and himself becoming their patron.

Joce de Dinan had already defected to the Angevins in 1141, bringing Ludlow Castle to their camp (both Joce and his wife had many relatives already in that faction). In 1144, Hugh became even more isolated when William de Braose also switched sides, taking control of Kingsland with him. The trigger for this was the conquest of Normandy by Geoffrey of Anjou, which forced lords to choose between their lands in Normandy or England. Interestingly, Hugh Mortimer chose to maintain his position in England, but the royal faction was now focused just on Wigmore and Richards Castle.

With Kingsland now on the Angevin side, key routes south were cut off. In response, in 1144 Hugh reconquered Maelienydd and rebuilt Cymaron Castle, which had been lost to the native Welsh rulers in the mid-1130s, whilst there were no Mortimers in the country, thus opening up alternative routes south (and in following years captured one Welsh prince and had him blinded, and killed another). To counter this, Roger, earl of Hereford (Miles' son) seized the castle and manor of Presteigne from Osbern fitz Hugh of Richards Castle, to disrupt Hugh's lines of communications between Wigmore and his Welsh territories. Having lost Presteigne, the lords of Richards Castle subsequently built themselves another castle at nearby Stapleton.

Photogrammetric view of Cymaron made from 43 individual drone photographs processed to construct a 3-D digital model and recoloured with red for the highest points (some tree tops), down to green. Some 'modern' buildings can be seen in the bailey (© CPAT image 1112-003, photograph by Julian Ravest)

After a few years of stalemate, by 1148 Earl Roger was preparing a major attack against the royal strongholds of Wigmore and Richards Castle. As Shobdon was in the frontline of such an attack, Hugh moved the canons of Shobdon Priory to Lower Lye in Aymestrey, leaving himself free to establish a castle at Shobdon – the site of the castle that he constructed can be seen just to the west of the church.

As part of William de Braose's defection to the Angevins he had agreed to pull down his castle at Kingsland to prevent it falling into the hands of Hugh Mortimer, whose position was now extremely dangerous as Wigmore and Richards Castle were completely surrounded – Kingsland, Pembridge, Little Hereford, Ludlow, Clun, Knighton, Presteigne and Kington were all controlled by supporters of the Angevins.

The attack didn't immediately materialise as Prince Henry (Matilda's son and now leader of the Angevins) landed in England to raise an army in the north. However, when Prince Henry returned to Normandy, Earl Roger was able to resume action against Hugh in 1149 and the Wigmore Chronicle records that Hugh was forced to remain behind closed doors in Wigmore Castle. There is evidence of a siege castle built by the earl against Hugh's castle at Shobdon (the motte south of the church).

Joce de Dinam in stained glass in St Laurence's Church, Ludlow

With the direct route from the south through Kingsland open to his enemies, Hugh decided in 1150 to again move the canons, this time from Aymestrey which lay on the direct route to Wigmore, to a site by Wigmore parish church, close to the safety of his own castle.

It appears that Hugh's response to this stranglehold was to seek to break out eastwards toward his castles at Cleobury Mortimer and Bridgnorth (a royal castle, but held by Ralph and Hugh for some years). To do this, Hugh needed to attack and lay siege to Joce de Dinan in Ludlow Castle.

The Wigmore Chronicle relates how war broke out between Hugh Mortimer and Joce de Dinan with Hugh laying siege to Ludlow Castle. Hugh, however, was captured and held prisoner in the castle until an enormous ransom of 3,000 silver marks (£2,000) was paid as well as plate, horses and birds. There is an old tradition that Hugh was imprisoned within what came to be called Mortimer's Tower in Ludlow Castle, but this tower was not actually built until a later date.

Nowadays, there is a quiet, unclassified back road between Wigmore and Ludlow, but this too gives us a glimpse into this period of feuding and violence between neighbours. In the space of a few miles there are four churches built under the patronage of the Mortimers: at Leinthall Starkes, Leinthall Earls, Elton and Pipe Aston – the latter is particularly notable for the engraved tympanum above the entrance door, which again is by the Herefordshire School of Romanesque Sculpture.

THE HEREFORDSHIRE SCHOOL OF ROMANESQUE SCULPTURE

On the inner tour, the work of the Herefordshire School of Romanesque Sculpture can be seen at three locations: St Giles', Pipe Aston where there is the tympanum above the entrance door and the font inside; the Shobdon Arches; and the font and carved dragon shaft at St George's, Orleton.

As mentioned in the main text, the new Norman rulers established their domination through building castles that stamped their authority on the land. They also established churches, priories and abbeys to demonstrate their piety and provide an insurance for the afterlife. There will have been great rivalry between the patrons of churches and, although village churches could not compete with the size and majesty of great cathedrals and abbeys, they could seek to outdo each other in the elaborate detail of the sculpture and decoration, which had been aided by the introduction of better tools.

The churches are a vivid reminder of how well-travelled the Normans were. Most Norman lords in the early twelfth century still owned lands and castles in Normandy, and regarded themselves as Norman rather than English. They travelled across the Channel to their estates, where business, family relationships, disputes and war would have taken them much further afield into France. Pilgrimage to famous sites such as Rome and Santiago de Compostela in Spain was common. Romanesque sculpture was a European revival of styles from the Roman period and analysis shows that ideas from across Europe were brought back and influenced the sculpture and decoration of churches in England.

The lords who commissioned church buildings employed masons and sculptors. Analysis of remaining sculpture has identified common themes and styles in a number of churches indicating the work of a single school (or workshop) of sculptors who were commissioned to work in Herefordshire and surrounding areas and whose work has been called the Herefordshire School of Romanesque Sculpture.

Analysis of the detail of this work has led experts to believe that there were two dominant sculptors who are referred to as the Chief Master and the Aston Master. The latter worked on the sculpture at St Giles', Pipe Aston and it is thought that they both worked together at Shobdon church.

Although it has often been assumed that the founding of the school was associated with Oliver de Merlimond's pilgrimage to Santiago de Compostela and the ideas that he brought back, this is not the case. Churches such as Kilpeck in south Herefordshire (which is the most complete example of their work) predate Oliver's pilgrimage of soon after 1136. Also, the Wigmore Chronicle recounts that Oliver had not only commissioned Shobdon church but also that building work had started before he departed.

Instead, it appears that both the Chief Master and the Aston Master were involved with and probably received their training a decade earlier at Hereford Cathedral, which played an important part in the development of the Herefordshire School. The work of the school is evident also in churches built in the late 1150s indicating that the school spanned a period of 30–35 years. Experts who have compared their work with similar sculpture across Europe have shown that the Herefordshire School used a wide range of ideas and sources drawn from western France, northern Italy, Spain and the Byzantine Empire, as well as local, native, Anglo-Saxon and Welsh influences. Combining a variety of styles and sources would have been seen as exotic, elite and prestigious.

Although Oliver de Merlimond cannot be credited with founding the school, Hugh Mortimer (d.1181–85) and Oliver were important patrons who commissioned the school to work on their projects, notably at Pipe Aston, Shobdon and Orleton. All the indications are that Oliver was well educated, had connections with scholars and churchmen in England and abroad and contributed ideas gained from his travels to the continuing development of the school.

> The tympanum above the north doorway of St Giles', Pipe Aston has been considered to be the first work of the Aston Master. The font is also a product of his work, though the carving is now upside down, suggesting that it is not serving its original function, which may have been as the base of a cross.
>
> The work of both the Chief Master and the Aston Master is evident at Shobdon. The church that Oliver commissioned was demolished and replaced in 1752, though the chancel arch and the north and south doorways were re-erected as a folly (the Shobdon Arches) a quarter of a mile away to the north at the end of a tree-lined avenue. Much of the detail is now lost due to weathering. The Romanesque font is preserved inside the current church.
>
> The font in St George's, Orleton is definitely by the school though experts feel that the figures lack the high quality of work elsewhere. In contrast the fragment of a carved shaft depicting a dragon, which originally would have decorated a chancel arch or doorway, is regarded to have been a high quality work. The two pieces indicate that the church was originally decorated more completely with sculptures from the school. It has been suggested that it is possible that the poorer quality of the Orleton font indicates that it was made after Oliver de Merlimond had left the employ of Hugh Mortimer and his advice on artistic matters was no longer available to Hugh.
>
> To find out more read: *The Herefordshire School of Romanesque Sculpture* (with a history of the Anarchy in Herefordshire by Bruce Coplestone-Crow) by Malcolm Thurlby, published by Logaston Press).

Unusually for such a small village, Pipe Aston also contains the sites of two castles. At the site of the first, by the church and referred to as the 'Pipe Aston Tump', the motte and bailey can be clearly seen. Its location suggests that its purpose was possibly to warn of attack from Ludlow and provide initial defence to the Wigmore estates, and would have been of use during the period of the Anarchy and the warring feuds between Hugh and Joce de Dinan. The second site further along the lane is much harder to discern and may have been a temporary siege castle set up to besiege the Mortimers' castle.

The Anarchy eventually came to an end in 1153 when, with the armies of King Stephen and Prince Henry facing each other across the Thames at Wallingford, the nobles on both sides forced them to settle for a truce. At

Winchester, the king and prince agreed a peace based on Stephen remaining king for his lifetime but recognising Henry as his heir (his own son having died), and the nobles of each faction swore fealty to both men. On the death of Stephen in 1154, Prince Henry duly became king and set out to restore law, order and royal authority.

As king, Henry II started by requiring that all former royal castles were surrendered to the Crown. Hugh Mortimer, possibly as someone who had been loyal to King Stephen, perhaps underestimating Henry and not realising fully that the period of anarchy had ended, defied the king and refused to give up Bridgnorth Castle. In 1155, Henry set out to assert his authority by devastating Hugh's estates and besieging his castles of Cleobury, Wigmore and Bridgnorth. The earthworks to the north-west and south-east of Wigmore Castle may be the remains of siege castles constructed by the king's army. When Wigmore and Cleobury fell, Hugh was forced to submit and surrender Bridgnorth, but was not otherwise penalised and was allowed to keep Wigmore, though Cleobury was destroyed.

It could be that this incident reflects the growing importance of the Mortimers in the region, in that having asserted his authority the king did not wish to further alienate a powerful local family. Indeed, it seems that the Mortimers had acquired certain unusual privileges which exempted them from military obligations to the Crown in relation to their estates in Shropshire. This gave the Mortimer lands in Shropshire a unique status and independence similar to those of the Marcher lords. The boxed information (pp. 18–20) explains that the name of Marcher lordships did not simply define a geographical area, far more importantly it indicated the almost royal powers that the lord exercised within them – powers that evolved over a long period. It took another 100 years until the Mortimers in the 1260s were able to secure Marcher status for the lordship of Wigmore itself.

Although Hugh lived for between a further 25 to 30 years there are very few records of what he did in his later life, though the tussles with the Welsh for control of Maelienydd continued, with the Welsh now regaining control. Indeed, Hugh was fined by the king for continuing a private war after Henry II had formally recognised the *status quo* in Wales, though the fine was never paid. He founded Wigmore Abbey when he moved the canons a final time. The site on the ridge by Wigmore parish church, that he had given to the canons who had been forced to move first from Shobdon and then Aymestrey, had proved to be unsuitable. Hugh now provided land a mile and a quarter from his castle, laid the first stone, paid the building costs and in 1179 had Wigmore Abbey dedicated by the bishop of Hereford. Hugh died soon after at Cleobury and was the first of many Mortimer lords of Wigmore to be buried at Wigmore Abbey.

Some contemporaries described Hugh as a man of 'extreme arrogance and presumption' and as being 'notable for pride and wrath'. Unsurprisingly, perhaps, the Wigmore Chronicle describes the abbey's founder as dying 'at a ripe old age and full of good works'!

Hugh was succeeded by his son, Roger Mortimer (d.1214). Unfortunately, Roger was in prison, and not for the last time in his life. The cause was the continuing struggle for control of Maelienydd. A prince from south Wales, Rhys ap Gruffudd, had come to dominate much of Wales and provide effective leadership against the Anglo-Norman barons. Hugh had lost much of his lands in Maelienydd and was unable to regain them as King Henry II had come to an agreement with Rhys, appointing him his justiciar of south Wales, and they had both recognised a Welsh chief, Cadwallon ap Madog, as ruler of Maelienydd. In 1179, Roger Mortimer's men killed Cadwallon when he was returning from court with a royal safe conduct. As a result, the king imprisoned Roger in Winchester, possibly for up to three years.

The remains of Wigmore Abbey

A few years later, in 1191 Roger was forced into exile from England. In the absence of Richard I (the Lionheart) on Crusade, Roger was accused of entering into an unexplained conspiracy with the Welsh against the king. The Justiciar of England, William Longchamp, besieged and captured Wigmore Castle and banished Roger. It may well be that Roger was involved in the plotting of the king's younger brother John, who was stirring up trouble against Richard. Certainly, Roger and the Mortimer family subsequently showed great loyalty to John, even when most others turned against him.

Within a few years of succeeding to the throne in 1199, King John managed to lose all the royal family's lands in France. In 1205, Roger Mortimer led an expeditionary force to Dieppe but was captured (again) and had to be ransomed by his wife.

One consequence of the defeats in France was that barons had to choose between their territories in England and France. For Roger Mortimer this was probably a straightforward decision. Apart from any loyalty to King John, the family's lands and wealth in England now well surpassed those in France.

Conflict with the Welsh continued during Roger's life, and in 1195 he had achieved total control over Maelienydd, including retaking the castle at Cymaron. Clearly, there were many casualties as he later made a grant to the abbey of Cwm Hir in Maelienydd in 1200, commemorating 'our men who died in the conquest of Maelienydd'. It has recently been convincingly argued that it was Roger Mortimer who probably commissioned the building of the great church at Cwm Hir, which had one of the longest naves in England and Wales. Roger was also briefly granted the castle of Knighton in 1207, although it was taken from him after a few months. Originally within the district of Maelienydd, Knighton had been an English borough and castle since the Conquest, but it now became another focus of contention between the Mortimers and the Welsh.

Shortly before his death in 1214, Roger resigned his honours in favour of his son and, on his death, was buried at Wigmore Abbey.

LEFT: Charter issued by Roger Mortimer (d.1214) to Abbey Cwm Hir in 1200 (*Archives of University College, London*). RIGHT: Nave of Abbey Cwm Hir church (one of the longest in England and Wales), probably commissioned by Roger Mortimer (© *CPAT image 4236-3411, photograph by Julian Ravest*)

THE WELSH MARCHES AND MARCHER LORDSHIPS

Although the Mortimers owned estates across England, they made Wigmore their principal residence and the centre – the *caput* – of their estates, taking their title as lords of Wigmore. Their reason for doing so could be that a lordship on the border with Wales offered opportunities for further conquest and a measure of independence.

After the Conquest, William I established three great earldoms – Hereford, Shrewsbury, Chester – to control the border area, and appointed at their head trusted comrades who were experienced war leaders. In turn, the earls began to appoint their own men to govern areas within their districts. This arrangement didn't last long as following generations rebelled (for example, Hereford in 1075) and lost their lands or died out. As a result, the lordships that had been created came to hold their lands directly from the king as tenants-in-chief.

As the frontier with the Welsh, the Marcher lordships provided not just a defensive barrier but were also allowed to take opportunities for personal conquest in Wales. The name Marcher comes from the Saxon word *mearc*, meaning border between two countries, and documents from this period increasingly refer to the Welsh Marches and recognise their unique status and powers: Magna Carta, for example, refers to the 'law of the Marches'.

The powers acquired during the twelfth and thirteenth centuries included the rights – restricted to their Marcher lands, so excluding any they held elsewhere in the kingdom – to raise their own armies and to wage private war in Wales, together with unlicensed castle-building. They also included 'the rights of the king' in terms of administering criminal and civil justice, meaning they could establish their own courts, appoint their own judges and, most importantly, collect the fines exacted by the courts. Crucially, the royal sheriffs had no power in the Marcher lordships. The lords could establish boroughs and grant charters of liberties, as well as other royal privileges such as salvage and treasure trove. The Marcher lords jealously guarded these powers and sought to expand them – one lord is quoted as claiming that the king's writ did not apply in his lands, and another, offended by the tone of a letter from the king, forced the king's messenger to eat the document including the seal. Not surprisingly, the Marcher lords sought to encroach this power eastwards by taking their neighbouring lands that they owned out of the royal shire system and into Marcher independence – Roger Mortimer (d.1282) seems to have done this successfully with his lordship of Wigmore in the 1260s and also his estates at Cleobury in Shropshire.

The extent of the Welsh Marches evolved during a period of over 200 years after the Conquest. As well as the borderlands, the area recognised as the Marches grew to include much of south Wales that had been conquered by the Normans. It was not until the final conquest of Wales by Edward I at the end of the thirteenth century that Wales and the Marches settled into a defined geography: north and west Wales became an area known as the Principality administered for the Prince of Wales or the Crown, whilst south and east Wales and the borders were by then divided into 50 or so Marcher lordships held directly from the king as tenants-in-chief.

The families who were Marcher lords changed considerably over the period due to families dying out or losing royal favour. The Mortimers were the only family to survive from before Domesday into the fourteenth century, let alone the fifteenth century, which is one reason for their emerging dominance. Furthermore, whilst in the early period after the Conquest their lands in the Welsh Marches were a strong focus for the Marcher lords and source of their wealth, by the fourteenth and fifteenth centuries this had changed. In 1200 only one Marcher lord, William the Marshal, was also an English earl, but 100 years later, in 1307, whilst seven out of ten earls of England held Marcher lordships, these were only a small part of their possessions. By the late fourteenth century, the Mortimers controlled one-third of the 50 or so Marcher lordships which formed the core of their wealth and power (see map on p. 52) . Although highly controversial at the time, it is not surprising that when he was raised to the rank of earl, Roger Mortimer (d.1330) chose the title 'earl of March'.

The Welsh Marcher lordships maintained their unique status until, during the reign of Henry VIII, they were integrated in 1536–42 into the administrative and governmental system of England. The powers of the Marcher lordships were abolished and, for administrative and judicial purposes, were subsumed into either the seven new counties of Wales or the existing English counties. Ludlow, though never a Marcher lordship, still retained an important role. After 1425, the Mortimer lands and titles passed through female descent to the duke of York, who made Ludlow his main base, and his son, Edward, was earl of March and lord of Ludlow. When he seized the throne and became Edward IV, Ludlow and all the Mortimer lands and titles became the property of the Crown. In 1473 Edward IV sent his eldest son and heir to be brought up in Ludlow, and created the Prince's Council based in Ludlow. When, some 60 years later, the Marcher lordships were abolished, the Council of the Marches based in Ludlow continued to administer Wales and the border counties, giving Ludlow the title of Capital of the Marches. The Council was abolished in 1689.

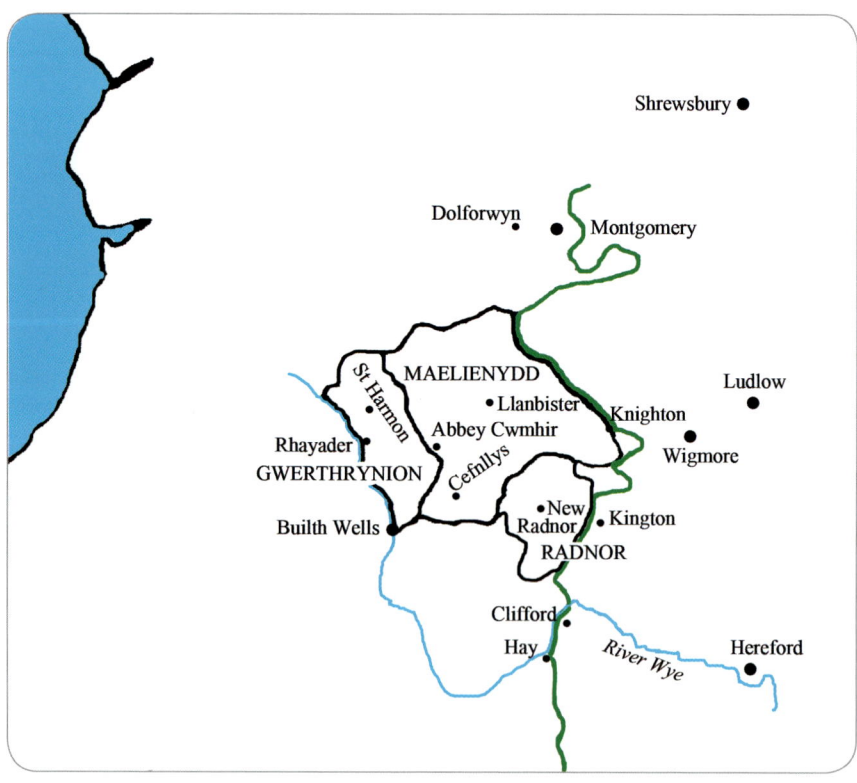

Map showing the locations of the lordships of Maelienydd and Gwerthrynion in central Wales, gained by the Mortimers through conquest, and that of Radnor through marriage (in 1247). The green line marks the approximate position of the current English-Welsh border

TWO

Consolidation and Expansion: 1214–1304

During the thirteenth century, marriage to wealthy and influential heiresses added significantly to the Mortimer estates, in the Welsh Marches as well as across England and Ireland; although during the century control of the Welsh conquests passed back and forth, by its end the English conquest of Wales was completed and the Mortimers were rewarded for their part with yet more lordships in the Marches. By the turn of the century, the Mortimers were amongst the wealthiest, most powerful and influential barons in the country. The period covers three generations: Hugh Mortimer (d.1227), his younger brother Ralph Mortimer (d.1246), Roger Mortimer (d.1282) and Edmund Mortimer (d.1304).

Hugh Mortimer (d.1227) succeeded his father in 1214 at a time of escalating unrest, confusion and violence in the kingdom. Increasingly, many of the barons had become exasperated and angry with King John's cruel nature and arbitrary rule, particularly as he became more expert at extorting money from them to pay for his wars and campaigns. The barons' discontent grew and fomented into open rebellion, which in 1215 led to the issuing of Magna Carta (see overleaf), whose terms represented King John's giving in to the barons' demands.

Throughout the turmoil, Hugh Mortimer, like his father, remained loyal to King John. In spring 1215 he assembled with other barons loyal to John and was rewarded with a gift of a valuable warhorse and estates in Gloucestershire. However, he was not present at Runnymede at the sealing of Magna Carta and it is only through a letter that lists the supporters of King John that we know that Hugh continued to be one of them. He attended the burial of King John at Worcester Cathedral in 1216, but was not among the 13 executors of John's will. As John was succeeded by his nine-year-old son, Henry III, the country was ruled by a regency council, of which Hugh was a member but not part of its inner circle. In 1225, he is one of the barons listed as witnessing the reissue of Magna Carta.

> **MAGNA CARTA: the Baronial Reform Movement and the Mortimers' role in the changing relationships between the king and the barons**
>
> An important theme during the medieval period was the changing relationship between the king, the barons and people's representatives in Parliament. Three major issues existed: the extent to which the king could act in an arbitrary manner or was subject to the law; the king's power to raise taxes; and what happened when there was a weak, ineffective or unpopular king.
>
> Increasingly, as the family became more powerful, Mortimers played a significant role in the evolving drama. Roger Mortimer (d.1282) became an influential military leader for the royal faction during the Barons' War; Roger Mortimer (d.1330) was instrumental in forcing the abdication of Edward II in 1326, then held enormous influence as virtual ruler before being executed for treason in 1330; within 40 years, marriage brought the Mortimers close to the succession to the Crown and they were caught up in intrigue and used as a focus for rebellion; a Mortimer grandson became king when he defeated the Lancastrian king in battle (and later had Henry VI killed).
>
> As recounted in the main text above, Roger (d.1214) and his son Hugh (d.1227) remained loyal to King John during and after the events that led to the issuing of Magna Carta. This set out the limitations of royal power, proclaimed the principle that the king is subject to the law, and established the rights of barons. The principle that taxation must be by consent became fixed in English politics, as did the principle that no free man could be imprisoned except by the lawful judgement of his peers.
>
> Within months King John sought release from its provisions by appeal to the Pope, who duly acquiesced on the grounds that John had been forced into signing it. The rebellion continued. When King John died in 1216 his son was only nine years old and England was on the brink of being taken over by France as Prince Louis was actively campaigning in England, having been invited by the rebellious barons to take the Crown.

With the death of John, the ground shifted as personal animosity towards the king was no longer an issue. When the barons loyal to the Crown reissued Magna Carta in 1216 in the name of the new king, Henry III, most of the barons abandoned Prince Louis, who returned to France. At the end of the wars in 1217 a further, less radical, version was issued, this time in conjunction with the Laws of the Forest. In 1225 Henry again reissued Magna Carta (Hugh Mortimer (d.1227) is listed as one of the witnesses), in return for taxation, and this became the definitive version. Originally referred to in 1215 as 'the Charter', by this time it had become known as the 'Great Charter' (thus Magna Carta).

Although not as unpleasant a character as his father, Henry III was not an effective monarch. The main text on pages 27–29 describes how the barons forced the king to agree to a set of reforms called the Provisions of Oxford in 1258, and the role of Roger (d.1282) in the disputes and wars that culminated in the Battle of Evesham in 1265. At one stage during the disputes, the barons led by Simon de Montfort had the king and royal family in custody. During a period of 18 months, Simon called Parliament to meet and, in addition to barons, he also invited representatives, for the first time, from all parts of England – knights from the shires, burgesses from towns and cities chosen by the people – to discuss matters of national concern.

Although, with the defeat of Simon in 1265, the controls on the king were removed, the reforms of local government that had been introduced were retained. On becoming king, Edward I continued to summon representatives of the shires and towns to Parliament.

Later sections in the main text describe how, just over 60 years later, Roger Mortimer (d.1330) was the main figure in what has been described as a totally 'new and revolutionary act in England' – the forced abdication of the king and his replacement by a new ruler (in this case the king's young son). The next 155 years saw two further kings deposed and killed – Richard II in 1399 following events triggered by the death of Roger Mortimer (d.1398); and Henry VI during the Wars of the Roses after Edward IV, a Mortimer grandson, won the Crown – and another disposed of before his coronation (the young Prince Edward, who disappeared whilst in the Tower of London after the death of Edward IV).

All this indicates that the Mortimers were still in the second rank of barons, but their loyalty to King John and his son Henry was beginning to bring them forward and they began to receive more royal favours. Certainly, before Hugh died in 1227 he was allowed to make his will despite owing the king the large sum of just over £1,015, a warhorse and two hawks.

Although it is recorded that the Mortimers now owned estates in 21 counties, much of Hugh's time was occupied in the Welsh Marches where there was yet another change of fortune. In 1215, the conquests of Roger (d.1214) in Maelienydd were reversed by Llywelyn ab Iorwerth (the Great), Prince of Gwynedd, who had come to dominate most of Wales and provide leadership against the Anglo-Norman incursions. Llywelyn captured and destroyed Knighton Castle, which had been held since 1207 by the Sheriff of Shropshire, and also destroyed Cymaron Castle which was never rebuilt. Hugh was unable to halt the current tide and Maelienydd and the castle and borough of Knighton remained in Welsh hands when he died from injuries sustained in a tournament on 10 November 1227. He was buried at Wigmore Abbey.

As Hugh had no children, he was succeeded by his younger brother Ralph Mortimer (d.1246), who remained focussed on Welsh matters and in the end was successful in re-establishing Mortimer power and influence. Initially, though, he could make no inroads, partly due to the power of Llywelyn and also the stand-off in English royal policy towards further incursions into Welsh-controlled territory.

In 1230, Ralph married Llywelyn's daughter, Gwladus Ddu, which proved an alliance of lasting significance in boosting the prominence of the Mortimer family. Llywelyn's approach was to secure marriages for his daughters into powerful Marcher families, despite, or indeed because of, the continual feuding with Marcher lords. Gwladus Ddu herself had been married first to Reginald de Braose, who had died in 1228. The de Braose family had earlier become one of the most powerful Marcher families with great strongholds in their lordships of Hay, Brecon, Abergavenny and Radnor (which included the manor and castle of Kingsland). At one time favourites of King John, he had turned on them and cruelly persecuted members of the family. Gwladus, though, may have had some say in the marriage to Ralph as Magna Carta had protected the status of widows by ensuring both their property rights and also that widows were free to marry whomever they wished or to choose to remain single (previously the king had often forced the widows of tenants-in-chief to remarry or taken large fines from them to remain single). It is likely, therefore, that the marriage of Ralph and Gwladus was one they both wanted – though whether for reasons of mutual advantage or love is harder to say.

Through this marriage, subsequent generations of Mortimers could claim to be descended from the Welsh princes of north Wales, and through them from the heroic King Arthur, whose line had descended through the princes of Wales (this was a period when Arthur was seen as an historical person and the histories of his deeds were being written). Ralph's repossession in 1230 of Knighton, which had been in the hands of Llywelyn, might have been because it formed part of Gwladus Ddu's dowry; the right granted to him in 1230 by Henry III to hold a fair there may also have been linked to the marriage. However, the rest of Maelienydd stayed in Llywelyn's hands and, despite the marriage, Ralph's relationship with his father-in-law remained very poor. It is possible that Llywelyn first built the castles at Cefnllys and Knucklas sometime between 1218 and 1234. With the death of Llywelyn in 1240, though, everything changed and by 1241 Ralph had regained control of his lands in Maelienydd, and is recorded as giving responsibility, whilst he himself was out of the country, to his young son, Roger, aged 11, to build castles at Cefnllys and Knucklas.

A view over the collapsed and stone-robbed remains of Knucklas Castle, built by Roger Mortimer in 1242, looking down the Teme Valley towards Knighton
(© CPAT image 4236-3410, photograph by Julian Ravest)

In 1230 the land and castle of Presteigne had also passed to Ralph as custodian of de Braose lands – the execution of William de Braose by Llywelyn for having an affair with his wife meant that the de Braose estates were to be split between his four daughters who were all young children. Mortimer control of the Presteigne lordship was cemented in 1247 when Ralph's son, Roger (d.1282) married Maud, one of the four de Braose heiresses. Although the castle was destroyed in 1262, Presteigne remained a Mortimer possession. The church of St Andrew in Presteigne has an interesting collection of possible Mortimer artefacts.

One measure of Ralph's success in expanding the Mortimer lands was that, the year after his death in August 1246, his 16-year-old son, Roger had to pay a large sum of 2,000 marks (£1,333) to compensate the Crown for the remaining rights of wardship – in effect to buy out the profits that the king could have made whilst controlling the estates until Roger was 21, when he would have formally come of age and could inherit and control his estates.

In the same year, although still a minor aged 16, Roger married Maud de Braose, a wealthy heiress twice over. On her father's side, as described above, she was a co-heir of William de Braose; from her mother she was a co-heir of the great lordship of the Marshal family, earls of Pembroke, which had also died out in the male line. The de Braose/Marshal inheritance added to the Mortimer holdings in the central Marches, notably with the de Braose lordship of Radnor which bordered Maelienydd on the south. The de Braose inheritance also brought one-third of the small lordship of St Clears in the south-west Marches. Together with the neighbouring lordship of Narberth, and one-third of the lordship of Haverford (both being Maud's share of the Marshal inheritance), this gave the Mortimers a presence in the south-west Marches.

In addition to Presteigne, the de Braose inheritance also included the manor and castle of Kingsland, where Maud and her successors oversaw the building of the current church, which still stands almost entirely as they built it. A coat of arms associated with Maud can be seen in the east window. The manor remained a Mortimer possession throughout and for a period they acted as direct patrons of the church, appointing the clergy, including two younger Mortimer sons as rectors in 1304 and 1315 (their names can be seen on the board in the church listing the parish's clergy).

Through his skills as a military leader and politician, Roger was able to use this new position and landed wealth to establish himself as one of the leading nobles in the country.

The first period of Roger's lordship from 1246 to 1265 was a time of confusion in both England and Wales, characterised by conflicting loyalties in response to changing circumstances.

At first the Mortimer loyalty to the Crown was tested as Roger's relationship with King Henry III and his powerful son, the Lord Edward (later King Edward I) became fraught. A number of issues contributed to this. First, the royal government was very slow and inefficient in distributing Maud's estates between the co-heirs on both sides of her family, so that Roger's share was not determined finally until 1259. Then the Crown took back the estates in Gloucestershire given to his father. Meanwhile a grandson of Llywelyn the Great, Llywelyn ap Gruffudd, again succeeded in uniting the Welsh, leading to renewed challenges to the Mortimers' hard-won lands in central Wales. Gwerthrynion was lost in 1256 and Maelienydd also in 1262, when men loyal to Llywelyn seized Cefnllys castle. Although Roger was able to retake the castle, it was then surrounded by Llywelyn's army, and, whilst Roger was confined there, Llywelyn destroyed a number of the castles in the region including Presteigne, Knighton and Knucklas which were never rebuilt.

Initially there was no response to this threat from the king, and when Henry did promise Roger 200 marks (£133) in gold to assist him in resisting Llywelyn, half was not paid. The tensions and frustrations had been exacerbated in 1260, when Llywelyn captured and destroyed the strategic town and castle of Builth which Roger Mortimer had been entrusted to hold on behalf of the Lord Edward. Although formally absolved of blame (Roger had been in London at the time pursuing his claim to the estates in Gloucestershire), many did indeed hold Roger responsible and it caused enmity between him and the Lord Edward for some time.

A major factor in the slow response in England to the increasing threat from Wales was the deteriorating political situation. A baronial faction had become increasingly disenchanted with Henry III's governance of the realm; a disenchantment that crystallised over issues of taxation for foreign ventures and the role of the king's foreign favourites into a movement for reform in the relationship between the king and the barons. At first, possibly because of his own strained relationships with the royal family, Roger was a strong supporter of reform. In the Westminster Parliament of April 1258, Henry III agreed that the governance of the realm should be reformed by 24 men, half of them chosen by himself and half by the barons. Roger was one of the 12 chosen by the barons to serve with the 12 chosen by the king. Before the group of 24 could begin work, Parliament met again in June and the reformers took more control. A panel drawn from the 24 appointed a new council for the king with 15 members, again including Roger. The council was to choose the king's chief ministers and control the whole running of central government – this was revolutionary. The Parliament also embarked on a wide series of reforms, which became known as the Provisions of Oxford, to address the grievances that had arisen.

To add to the confusing mix of loyalties and relationships, the Lord Edward, despite being the king's son and heir, sided with the reformers. However, his enmity towards Roger Mortimer over the loss of Builth in 1260 opened the door for the king to win Roger back to his side (a process which involved numerous gifts). By the end of 1261 the king had formally pardoned Roger for his involvement in the barons' movement.

Another factor in the shifting loyalties was the growing feud between Roger and the leader of the barons, Simon de Montfort, who had earlier been granted land in the Marches. In 1263, the king (no doubt, in order to foment trouble) gave Roger three of Simon's manors in Herefordshire, which Roger promptly devastated. In retaliation, in February 1264, as relationships between the king and Simon deteriorated, Simon sent his sons to attack Mortimer estates, besieging Wigmore Castle. In the same year, Simon's army combined with the Welsh to seize and burn Radnor Castle.

Radnor Castle looking west (© CPAT image 4236-3409, photograph by Julian Ravest)

The Lord Edward, having broken with Simon and the barons, returned to the royal side in the dispute, and bitter fighting ensued between the two sides. Roger Mortimer played a leading role in the capture of the de Montfort stronghold of Northampton in April 1264. A month later, though, defeat at Lewes resulted in the loss of large numbers of the royal army and to the capture of the royal family by Simon. Roger Mortimer and other Marcher lords were allowed to return home to counter the growing threat posed by Llywelyn in Wales. Further disputes led to Simon again attacking the Marches in late 1264, capturing castles (including Wigmore), and putting Mortimer estates to the torch. As events developed in 1265, support for Simon de Montfort began to crumble, and on 28 May Roger engineered the Lord Edward's escape from confinement at Hereford, and together they fled to Wigmore and from there to Ludlow. This effectively cemented the friendship between Edward and Roger Mortimer, which was to continue when Edward became king.

Shortly after, in August 1265, the civil war culminated in the Battle of Evesham, when Roger commanded one of the three divisions of the Royalist army and, according to one account, personally killed Simon de Montfort. The Battle of Evesham was described at the time as 'the Murder of Evesham for battle it was not', and the slaughter continued in towns and churches as no sanctuary was given. This was highly unusual as it was very rare for nobles to be killed in battle (it was more profitable to capture and ransom them), but at Evesham Simon and 30 others were done to death when they could no longer go on fighting. Feelings had run so high, the feuds so personal and bitter, that they overruled all else. Indeed, Simon de Montfort's body was butchered and his severed head delivered to Wigmore Castle as a present and trophy for Roger's wife, Maud!

At this point the manor and castle of Pembridge came into Mortimer control. Since 1100 it had been owned by the de Pembridge family, but as a result of their support for Simon de Montfort, all their lands were confiscated and handed over to Roger Mortimer. Although their lands were later restored to them, Roger forced them to sign Pembridge over to the Mortimers permanently (done 'willingly' in court by Henry de Pembridge, while Roger held his sons captive!). On his death in 1282 at Kingsland Castle, his widow Maud lived at Pembridge which was to become part of the landholdings of Mortimer widows (Margaret de Fiennes 1304–33 and Joan de Geneville 1333–56) in the following century.

The site of Pembridge motte, with the church to its north in the background
(Photograph © Robert Anderson)

Although the loss of the Mortimer lands in Wales was confirmed by the Treaty of Montgomery in 1267, Roger Mortimer's support of the king, his friendship with the king's son and his military success made him a great power in England.

Roger appears to have used this position to strengthen his powers (to the exclusion of royal power) within his estates. A year after the Battle of Evesham he was granted a charter concerning his estates of Cleobury and Chelmarsh in Shropshire, uniting them into a single manor independent of aspects of royal law. Roger, though, twisted the meaning of this charter to give it a much wider scope, including more estates and turning them into an independent Marcher lordship. At the same time, he began a similar process at Wigmore and Radnor, excluding royal officers and claiming exemption from royal writs, taxes and the authority of justices, thus withdrawing them from the royal jurisdiction of England and turning them into Marcher lordships. The fact that he was allowed to get away with this indicates his value to the Crown.

When Edward, still as heir to the throne, went on Crusade in 1270, Roger Mortimer was one of those chosen as trustees for his children and estates. When Henry III died in 1272 with Edward still abroad, those trustees, especially Roger and two others, were virtual regents for two years, administering and governing the country until Edward returned in August 1274. The Treaty of Montgomery contained a number of ambiguities, one of which related to Roger Mortimer, Maelienydd and Cefnllys. The Treaty allowed Roger Mortimer to repair or rebuild the castle at Cefnllys, whilst Llywelyn could reclaim castle and land if he could demonstrate his right to it in court. The castle at Cefnllys stood at the northern end of a long ridge, but instead of repairing this castle, Roger built a new, larger castle at the southern end of the ridge, which led to complaints to the Crown by Llywelyn. He also complained that nothing was done to follow through on giving him an opportunity to argue his claim to the castle and land. Not surprisingly, with Roger Mortimer prominent in the government, this fell on deaf ears.

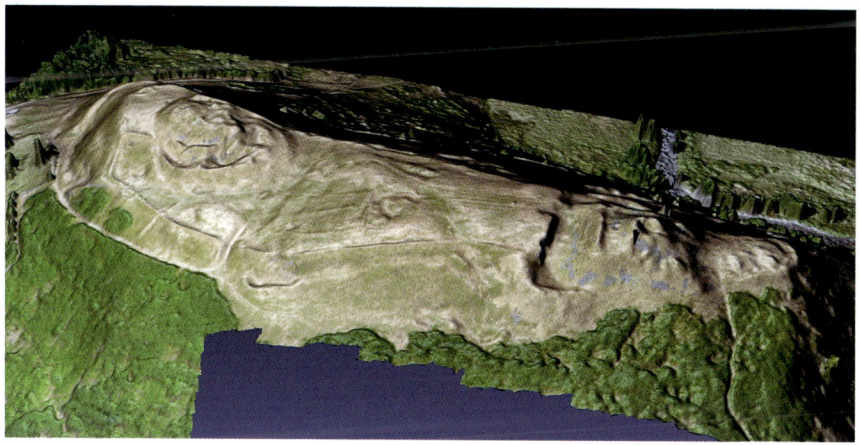

Photogrammetric image of Cefnyllys, showing the first castle at the north end of the ridge, on the left (© CPAT image 4236-3417, photograph by Julian Ravest)

On his return and newly crowned as king, one of Edward's priorities was to exert his overlordship of Llywelyn ap Gruffudd. He therefore required Llywelyn to give his fealty, but Llywelyn first prevaricated then refused, partly due to the harassment and encroachment on what he saw as his lands by Marcher lords, including Roger Mortimer. This refusal gave King Edward the cause to take up arms against Llywelyn in 1276/7.

Roger was appointed to lead one of the three armies assembled to assault Wales, his army striking into the central regions of Wales around and to the north of Maelienydd. In 1277 they besieged and captured Llywelyn's new castle at Dolforwyn, near Montgomery, contributing significantly to his overall defeat.

Dolforwyn Castle, first built by Llywelyn ap Gruffudd and rebuilt by Roger Mortimer (d.1282)

Two years later, in 1279, Roger was awarded with the lordships of Ceri and Cedewain, which included Dolforwyn castle. Although Roger rebuilt the castle at Dolforwyn, he immediately transferred the borough that Llywelyn had founded outside the castle down to a new, and more appropriate site in the valley bottom. The new town became known as Newtown, which it still is.

The defeat of the Welsh in 1277 had also enabled Roger to regain possession of Maelienydd. To cement his control, Roger built a new castle in the north-west of the district in a commanding position overlooking the valley of the river Ithon, where the strategic access route from the north cuts through a steep-sided gorge (now the route of the A483). Tinboeth castle is also known as Dinbaud (Maud's Castle) suggesting that Maud de Braose, Roger's wife, may have been involved in the establishment of the castle. Combined with the lordships and estates in the Marches brought to him through his marriage to Maud, the Mortimers were now the greatest of the Marcher lords (a position helped by other great families dying with no male heirs and the lands being split between surviving daughters).

Roger 'retired' in 1279, celebrating with a great tournament at Kenilworth which he called a 'round table' (a hint to his Arthurian pretensions). Although his military commission was renewed for Edward's final conquest of Wales in 1282, Roger soon fell ill and died at Kingsland in October 1282 and was buried at Wigmore Abbey. After the enmity over the loss of Builth had been overcome, the friendship between Roger and King Edward had endured for nearly 20 years. Indeed, on Roger's death the king wrote to one of his younger sons, another Roger:

LEFT: Aerial view of Tinboeth Castle, possibly built by Maud de Braose. RIGHT: The only standing remnant of the castle (© CPAT images 962-002 & 962-003, both photographs by Julian Ravest)

> As often as the king ponders over the death of [your] father he is disturbed and mourns the more his valour and fidelity, and his long and praiseworthy services to the late king and to him recur frequently and spontaneously to his memory. As it is certain that no one can escape death, the king is consoled, and [you] ought to be consoled on his part, because there is good hope that [your] father after the trials of this life has now a better state than he had.

Roger Mortimer had become one of the wealthiest men in England, whilst his military skills and friendship with King Edward had given him enormous influence and power well beyond the experience of previous generations of the family.

A few months before his death, the king had granted to that younger son, (the recipient of the letter above), the lordship of Chirk, which had been formed from lands confiscated from the native rulers of northern Powys. Henceforth, he became known as Roger Mortimer of Chirk (d.1326). The grant of Chirk to a younger son extended the power of the Mortimers into the northern Marches and made Roger Mortimer of Chirk a Marcher lord in his own right. Work to build an imposing new castle at Chirk started in the 1290s. His standing was further enhanced when his mother gave him some of the lands that she had inherited in the south-west Marches – the lordship of Narberth, and the one-third shares in the lordships of Haverford and St Clears (as his share of the latter bordered Narberth it was now subsumed into that lordship). Roger became a powerful baron, being appointed Justiciar of both north and south Wales.

TOP LEFT, Narberth Castle (© John Fleming) and LEFT, Haverfordwest Castle (© Paul R. Davis) were part of the inheritance of Maud de Braose, which she gave to her younger son, Roger Mortimer of Chirk. ABOVE, Chirk Castle, built by Roger Mortimer of Chirk after he was given the lordship of Chirk

Roger's wife, Maud de Braose, was a formidable woman in her own right. During her husband's lifetime, he was clearly happy to leave her in control of Wigmore and other lordships while he was absent. It was Maud who organised the defence of Wigmore when it was besieged by the armies of Simon de Montfort. And, when Roger took custody of Clun in 1267 on behalf of his widowed daughter and her infant son, he gave the custody to his wife, Maud. Various correspondence shows her to be resident there and co-ordinating networks of information about the activities of Llywelyn ap Gruffudd. When

Aerial view of Clun Castle, looking south-east, where Maud de Braose defied the sheriff of Shropshire (© Paul R. Davis)

Roger Mortimer died in 1282, as usual his lands were seized by the sheriff pending the inquisition to determine their settlement. When the sheriff of Shropshire arrived at Clun, the castle was held by Maud who refused him entrance and shouted insults from the tower. When the sheriff complained to the king, he received a royal command to stop molesting Maud!

Maud outlived her husband by 19 years before she died in 1301. During this period, she was assiduous in protecting the interests of the Mortimer family, particularly instigating numerous court cases in her own name, which, as a widower, she could do. One long-running series of court cases sought to protect the Mortimer interests in the district of Elfael to the south of Maelienydd. During the 1240s, as her husband, Roger had begun to assert a Mortimer claim to Elfael as Maud was one of the heiresses of the de Braose family that had seized it in the twelfth century. Although his claims were unsuccessful, in 1257 the Lord Edward granted his royal rights in northern Elfael to Roger Mortimer. Three years later, though, Llywelyn ap Gruffudd gained control of northern Elfael in 1260, and Painscastle in southern Elfael was surrendered to him by the Treaties of Pipton (1265) and Montgomery (1267). During the campaigns of Edward I in 1277, Roger Mortimer seized Elfael; however, a subsequent royal inquisition decided that the Tosny family were the lawful owners of Painscastle and the southern half, but that Roger, as the heir of the de Braose family, was the rightful owner of Colwyn and the northern half. When Roger Mortimer died in 1282, northern Elfael came under the control of his widow Maud. However,

 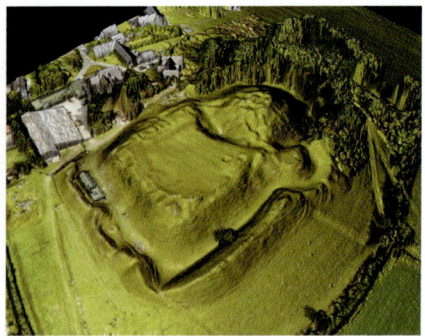

LEFT: Aerial view of Colwyn Castle, claimed by Roger Mortimer (© Paul R. Davis).
RIGHT: Photogrammetric image of Painscastle, also claimed by Roger Mortimer
(© CPAT image 4236-3418, photograph by Julian Ravest)

Ralph Tosny initiated legal claims to assert his rights to northern Elfael, and though Maud contested this in a long drawn-out, complicated and protracted round of legal disputes, eventually it must have been decided in favour of Tosny, as in 1292 Maud was recorded as holding nothing in Elfael.

Shortly after the death of Roger, his eldest son and heir, Edmund (d.1304), together with his younger brother, Roger of Chirk, were closely involved in the circumstances surrounding the death of Llywelyn ap Gruffudd in December 1282. Holed up in Snowdonia, Llywelyn, with a small army, broke out and proceeded to the central Marches, where he was killed in a skirmish near Builth. The two Mortimer brothers were present at the skirmish and may have been involved in luring Llywelyn into a trap. Llywelyn's severed head was sent to the king, and according to one tradition his body was buried at Abbey Cwm Hir.

Roger was succeeded by his second son, Edmund Mortimer (d.1304). As a younger son, Edmund had been trained for a career in the Church, but became heir to the Mortimer inheritance on the death of his older brother in 1274.

Edmund's time as lord of Wigmore was uneventful – certainly when compared to the achievements of his father and the dramatic career to come of his son. Unlike his father and grandfather, Edmund's marriage did not bring new estates and wealth to the Mortimers. With the final conquest of Wales achieved by Edward I, there was no more scope for ambition on that front. In England, Edmund played little role in national affairs and his relationship with King Edward appears from the records to have been slightly strained – possibly because Edmund presumed on the friendship between the king and his father; possibly because he did not have the leadership skills of his father.

THREE

King in Name or King of Folly: 1304–30

This section tells the story of just one member of the Mortimer dynasty – Roger Mortimer (d.1330). More than any other member of the family this Roger left his mark on both the affairs of the country and the locations on this tour (commissioning extensive building works at Wigmore Castle and church, Ludlow Castle, Leintwardine and Pembridge churches). He led such an eventful and colourful life that it is possible to give only the briefest summary in this section. Through inheritance, he owned vast estates in three countries; through marriage he added even more land, wealth and castles (including Ludlow); through ability, he became a key military commander and royal administrator; through circumstances, he was pushed into rebellion, imprisoned, condemned to death; through daring, he escaped to the Continent, lived in exile, and became the lover of the queen, before returning to force the abdication of the king and effectively rule the country for nearly four years; through ambition, he brought more Marcher lordships into the possession of the Mortimers, and added more wealth and titles, raising the family to the rank of earls; through over-reaching himself, he was executed as a traitor.

On the death of his father in July 1304, Roger Mortimer (d.1330) was only 17 years old. As a minor he had to pay a fine (this time 2,500 marks, or £1,666) to compensate Piers Gaveston, the nobleman and favourite of the king's son, who had been granted wardship of Roger.

At an even younger age, 14, Roger had married Joan de Geneville, aged 15, who was heiress to half of Ludlow (including the castle, which was to become a favourite Mortimer residence), manors in Shropshire, half the Marcher lordship of Ewyas Lacy, and large estates in Ireland, including the castle of Trim.

Longtown Castle in the lordship of Ewyas Lacy: the main gate with the round keep visible beyond (© Paul R. Davis)

The wedding between Roger and Joan in September 1301 took place at the church in Pembridge. Apart from two arches in the chancel and the south window in the chancel, that building no longer exists. The current church, though, was rebuilt with Mortimer money in the early 1330s.

In 1306, Roger was knighted alongside Prince Edward (the future King Edward II) and nearly 300 other young men at a splendid ceremony at Westminster. The following year he was called to Parliament for the first time and in 1308, following the death of Edward I, he was one of the four bearers of the royal robes at the coronation of Edward II.

In 1314, Roger led 300 men from his estates in the Marches into battle at Bannockburn, when Robert Bruce, King of Scotland, defeated a great English army to secure the independence of Scotland. It is not known for sure what role Roger played in the battle but it is possible that at the end he fought in a desperate rearguard action to protect the flight of the king. Roger was captured and, as a prominent noble who was third cousin to Robert Bruce, taken to the King of Scotland. Rather than being ransomed he was tasked with taking King Edward's privy seal and the royal shield, both captured on the battlefield, back to the English king. He also took the corpses of two other English nobles.

The early part of his career, however, was dominated by activity in Ireland. Although the Mortimers, through the marriage of his grandfather to Maud de Braose, had owned estates in Ireland for 60 years, in 1308 Roger became the first known head of the family to make a visit to the country. His own marriage to Joan had made him one of the principal lords of Ireland. Roger and Joan took an active interest in their affairs there, with Roger returning on a number of occasions and Joan accompanying him at least twice.

Roger suffered a setback in 1315 when war broke out in Ireland. Some leaders of Irish family and tribal groups, in an attempt to cast off the English yoke, had invited help from Robert I (Bruce), King of Scotland, who sent over his brother, Edward, at the head of an army. Roger was defeated in a battle at Kells and forced to return to England. However, in 1316 Roger was appointed King's Lieutenant of Ireland, with responsibility for defeating Edward Bruce. He returned to Ireland with a large army in 1317 and was successful in re-establishing English control of much of the country, with Edward Bruce being defeated and killed shortly after Roger returned to England in 1318.

Roger was appointed Justiciar of Ireland in 1319 and proved an able leader and administrator – when he was recalled in September 1320, the citizens of Dublin are recorded as commending his efforts 'in saving and keeping the peace'.

The pursuit of his family interests in Ireland combined with his administrative roles on behalf of the Crown had kept Roger apart from the growing tensions and disputes in England. Edward I had been an extremely strong-willed king who stamped his authority on the nobles. In contrast, his son, Edward II, was a much weaker character prone to strong attachments to particular individuals and allowing them to heavily influence him. An earlier crisis in his reign had sprung from the influence of Piers Gaveston, which led to the execution of Piers by a group of nobles, which the king never forgot nor forgave.

On his first return to England from Ireland in 1318, Roger had begun to be involved in the poisonous politics and relationships that had developed. He took part in the negotiations between the king and his opponents in 1318, became a member of the subsequent standing council of 16 and was placed on a commission appointed to reform the royal household. In return, Roger received a range of favours and gifts, further enhancing his wealth.

On his next return in 1320, though, the political situation had worsened considerably and this time Roger had no choice but to take sides and be drawn in. The king was now under the growing influence of the Despenser family, father and son, who were both named Hugh. With a well-deserved reputation for unscrupulous greed, the Despensers were exploiting their position as royal favourites to accumulate estates and lordships in the southern Welsh Marches, posing a direct threat to the Mortimer interests. In addition, the Despensers had a personal feud with the Mortimers as Roger (d.1282) had killed the head of their family at the Battle of Evesham in 1265, and they were seeking revenge.

Inevitably, Roger, along with the other Marcher lords, joined the opposition to the Despensers and were, therefore, in alliance against the king. In May 1321, Roger led a five-day rampage through the Despenser lordships in south Wales. At this point Edward II gave way and the Despensers were exiled. However, shortly afterwards the king engineered a pretext to annul the exile and resume hostilities. At the start of 1322, Roger was forced to surrender at Shrewsbury. Together with his uncle, Roger Mortimer of Chirk, Roger was sent to the Tower of London, tried and condemned to death. The sentences were subsequently reduced to terms of life imprisonment.

On 1 August 1323, having drugged the guards, Roger escaped and fled to France where his presence was accepted by the French king, brother of Edward's queen, Isabella. To give thanks for his escape, which was on the feast day of St Peter in Chains, Roger later built a chapel at Ludlow Castle, dedicated to St Peter, the ruins of which can be seen in the outer bailey (it is not the unusual round chapel sited in the inner bailey).

> **BISHOP ADAM OF ORLETON**
>
> One supporter and ally of Roger, who was said to have organised his escape from the Tower and was prominent in orchestrating the deposition of Edward II, was Adam of Orleton (c.1275–1345). It is not clear whether Adam was born in the village of Orleton or into a family of Orletons in Hereford. He studied for a career in the church, gaining a number of prominent positions, including in the papacy, where he became a close colleague of popes, and being entrusted to lead several diplomatic missions on behalf of the king.
>
> Adam became bishop of Hereford in 1317 and was closely associated with Roger. In 1322, the king removed Adam's income and wrote to the Pope to ask that he be removed from his bishopric and exiled – a request that was refused. Following Roger's escape he was accused of providing arms and horses for the enterprise. On Roger's return, Adam preached powerful sermons denouncing Edward II as being unfit to rule and became a member of the Regency Council and Treasurer in 1327, then Bishop of Worcester in 1328 and finally Bishop of Winchester in 1333 until his retirement and death at Farnham in Surrey.

INSIGHTS INTO THE LIFE OF A NOBLEMAN AND HIS WIFE

When Roger Mortimer (1287–1330) surrendered to the king in 1322 he forfeited not just his lands and titles but everything he and his wife, Joan, owned, including their clothing. An inventory of their belongings was made at Wigmore Castle and Abbey (Joan was then living at the abbey, possibly due to rebuilding work at the castle; Roger had also stored there his more valuable possessions). This long and detailed inventory gives a remarkable insight into the everyday lives of Roger and his wife. Only some details are given here, based on Dr Mortimer's description in his biography of Roger.

Roger's possessions at Wigmore Castle

- A large amount of war machinery – 6 siege engines, machines for flinging rocks and massive bolts, 21 windlass-operated crossbows, and 18 foot-operated ones, 291 crossbow bolts
- A large quantity of armour for jousting including 9 helmets and 1 'jousting coronet'
- War armour including a war helmet, 2 suits of plate armour, 2 helmets with visors and older items such as leather breastplates, suits of body armour, iron and leather helmets
- Collections of lances and shields, lance-shafts and lance-heads, pavilions and tents
- Some war memorabilia such as a Saracen crossbow and arrows, an Irish axe
- Hunting tools – drums, snares and nets
- A chessboard painted gold
- A gaming board made of aromatic nutmeg
- A number of practical everyday items – chests, coffers, benches, barrels

Roger's possessions at Wigmore Abbey

- A large amount of personal armour of very high quality
- Roger's personal wardrobe – 2 short jackets of green velvet, a range of tunics in different cloth and colours such as scarlet, velvet mulberry brown, green, hoods and hats
- A green bedcover embroidered with owls with 4 matching hanging carpets
- A bedcover with a blue background with several coats of arms embroidered, with 3 matching hangings
- A bedcover of knotted work, with 4 matching hangings
- A great hanging tapestry for a hall embroidered with popinjays and griffons
- 2 yellow hangings, old and made into curtains
- A hanging of good and subtle work with 4 matching ones
- A long benchcover striped yellow and red
- A large amount of cloth
- A brass horn together with a sword associated with the charter of the lands of Wigmore

> **JOAN'S POSSESSIONS AT WIGMORE ABBEY**
> - One wall hanging, four carpets, and a benchcover with the Mortimer coat of arms
> - 8 carpets
> - 3 chequered bedcovers
> - 1 red bedcover
> - 1 mattress covered with fine linen
> - 2 mattresses covered with canvas
> - 8 blankets
> - A range of bed linen
> - Pairs of curtains in muslin and linen
> - 4 tunics of different cloth and colour
> - 8 supertunics of different cloth and colour
> - A mantel and a hat without fur
> - New fur for a supertunic and a hood
> - Cloth for 3 altar cloths
> - 1 table cloth for a dinner table
> - 2 double towels
> - 3 small towels
> - 22 ells of linen cloth
> - 1 long towel
> - 3 table undercloths
> - 2 wool cushions of stitched work
> - 1 psalter
> - 4 books of romances
> - A chest containing – 2 striped red velvet cloths, 1 comb, 1 ivory mirror, 1 small ivory image of the Virgin Mary, 1 ivory scourge, 1 belt decorated with enamel and precious stones belonging to one of her daughters
> - A 2nd chest containing – 1 enamelled mirror, 1 set of ivory chessmen, an empty strongbox, 2 washbasins, 2 silver basins, 6 silver dishes, 4 silver salt cellars and 2 silver cups

In England, Edward II's fixation on and favouritism toward the Despensers had the effect of alienating his wife, Isabella, who was increasingly isolated from the king and demeaned by the Despensers. Isabella was the sister of the king of France, and Edward allowed her to lead a diplomatic mission to her brother's court in 1325. Once she was there, Edward permitted their young son and heir to the throne, Prince Edward, to join her. Control of their son and heir allowed Isabella more freedom of action, and she openly came out against her husband and the Despensers, refusing to return to England. A close friendship developed between Roger and Isabella, and by 1326 it was claimed in England that they were lovers. They developed a scheme to invade England, and in September 1326 landed in Suffolk with a small army. The hatred of the Despensers had become ever more intense and many came to support Isabella, as queen, and Roger as her military commander. Within weeks they were successful and the king himself was captured. In January 1327, Edward II was forced to agree to abdicate in favour of his young son.

For the next four years, Roger was at the height of his powers, influence and wealth; whilst, alongside Queen Isabella, he was the dominant figure in England.

Initially, Roger and Isabella were ruthless to their immediate enemies, overseeing and participating in the trials and cruel executions of the Despensers and other nobles.

The fate, though, of the captured Edward II remains a controversial topic. In 1327, relatives and supporters of Roger announced that the king had died in captivity at Berkeley Castle, of natural causes, and the body was buried at Gloucester. Afterwards, stories began to emerge that Roger Mortimer had ordered the murder of the king – stories which became ever more lurid and included the use of a red-hot poker, which is almost certainly untrue. Indeed, recent academic research has revealed a growing body of both direct and indirect evidence that Edward II did not die at Berkeley, that the body buried at Gloucester in 1327 was not his, and that he lived first in captivity at Corfe Castle in Dorset and then in exile on the Continent for at least another 15 years. The evidence for this is detailed in the books by Dr Ian Mortimer and Kathryn Warner, listed in the further reading.

Regardless of the fate of Edward II, Roger and Isabella did much else to provoke the resentment and animosity of the nobles. Roger made a critical mistake in not having an official position in the governance of the country – he was never officially regent, nor was he ever a member of the council established to direct the government during the minority of Edward III. Instead he used his relationship with the queen and the young king, and worked through allies such as Bishop Adam of Orleton, to appoint his allies to the great posts of the kingdom and to manipulate and control events.

In 1328, Roger was raised to the rank of earl. Given his vast estates and lordships, his relationship with the queen and the young king, and his role in ruling the country, this was not surprising. What did surprise people, however, was the title that he chose, earl of March, as there was no precedent for this.

THE CARVED STONE HEADS IN ST GEORGE'S, ORLETON

With buildings that are 600–900 years old it is not surprising that there are few surviving written records. It is also not surprising that over the generations people have tried to fill in the gaps and local traditions have developed. One such local tradition relates to the carved stone heads in St George's, Orleton. The six carvings are of male and female royals, a lord and two mitred churchmen, with a smaller carving above and to one side of the male royal. It is extremely tempting, therefore, to conclude that they represent the dramatic events recounted above of the life of Roger Mortimer (d.1330) and their connections to Orleton. In this scenario, the carvings represent King Edward II; his close friend Piers Gaveston; his wife Queen Isabella; the queen's lover, Roger Mortimer, who helped her to overthrow and depose the king in favour of her son; Bishop Adam of Orleton, as a supporter of Roger and the queen; and the Abbot of Wigmore Abbey.

However, recent scholarly analysis of the carvings by Dr Ian Mortimer leads to a different conclusion when they are assessed in the context of when they were carved, what was happening at the time, and comparison to other representations of those characters. An important starting point is that it is very unlikely that anyone in Orleton at that time would have paid for a carving of Piers Gaveston. Dr Ian Mortimer writes:

> The fourteenth-century modifications to Orleton parish church incorporate several sculpted heads. A local legend has sprung up associating these with famous characters of Edward II's reign, including Edward II, Queen Isabella and Roger Mortimer, 1st earl of March. However, there is no evidence for these identifications and they are chronologically problematic. The sculptures almost certainly date to the early years of the reign of Edward III, as indicated by the style of the work and the unbearded head of the king on the north wall. The unpainted head above the king's depicts an unidentified layman, possibly a local benefactor to the church. Opposite them on the south wall is the head of Edward III's queen, Philippa of Hainault.
>
> The heads on the arch are harder to identify. The head at the top probably represents a lord of Orleton manor, and this may well be Roger Mortimer, 1st earl of March (d.1330), as the manor was held by his widow, Joan, until her death in 1356. The bishops' heads (one on either side) probably represent two bishops of Hereford but which ones is unknown. One possibility is that they represent Thomas Charlton (bishop 1327–44), who was raised to the bishopric

due to the influence of Roger Mortimer, and whose nephew married Maud Mortimer (Roger and Joan's daughter) and an earlier bishop of Hereford, such as St Thomas de Cantilupe, who was canonised in 1320. However, another possibility is that the work was undertaken after the death of Adam of Orleton (d.1345), who was bishop of Hereford 1317–27, and later bishop of Worcester and finally bishop of Winchester. According to this theory, the heads depict him and his nephew, John Trilleck, who was bishop of Hereford when Orleton died. Adam of Orleton rose to great prominence in the affairs of England in alliance with Roger Mortimer. This theory would thus explain why the royal heads are included in this church along with those of two bishops and his patron, and might suggest that the unpainted layman is supposed to be the father of Adam of Orleton or another kinsman. However, it should be noted that Adam of Orleton's most recent biographer believes he was from Hereford, not Orleton.

What can be said without doubt is that the carved heads are a fascinating insight into life nearly 700 years ago and it would be interesting to track down when the local tradition first started.

It is also worth noting the many stone heads in St Mary's, Pembridge, which were carved at about the same time as the Orleton ones and which show some similarities of feature. A further similarity is the analysis and speculation as to who they are supposed to represent! (Photographs © Robert Anderson)

All earldoms related to specific counties, never before a whole region. This reflected not only Roger's ambition but also his recognition that the Mortimers' power derived from their dominance of the Marches. As well as titles, Roger accumulated more lands in England, Wales and Ireland, as well as a number of lucrative positions.

During the period of his ascendancy, Roger Mortimer, 1st earl of March, ensured that he acquired further Marcher lordships. In collaboration with Queen Isabella, he was granted the lordship of Denbigh, thus extending Mortimer influence further into the northern Marcher lordships. Next, he was granted Montgomery, for a rent of 85 marks, initially for the period of his life; in 1330, the grant was extended to a hereditary right to himself and his legitimate heirs in perpetuity. A similar deal was done for the lordship of Builth when, after he had first been appointed constable, Queen Isabella, with the agreement of Edward III, granted Builth Castle to him in 1329 for a rent of £113 6s 8d a year, payable to her for life. Furthermore, Edward III also granted Roger the reversion of the castle in perpetuity, which had been due to the Crown after Queen Isabella's death. In the final months of his rule, Roger was granted the lordship and castle of Clifford.

Builth Castle from the south-east (© Paul R. Davis). Seized by Llywelyn ap Gruffudd when his grandfather was the constable, it was granted to Roger Mortimer, 1st earl of March

LEFT TO RIGHT: Denbigh Castle (© Paul R. Davis); Montgomery Castle; Clifford Castle, which were all granted to Roger Mortimer during his ascendancy

Although his uncle, Roger Mortimer of Chirk (who had died in the Tower in 1326, shortly before his nephew's triumphant return) was survived by his son, Roger effectively disinherited his cousin by claiming that he was the heir of Roger of Chirk. Thus, he took possession of Chirk, though after his execution in 1330 it reverted to the Fitzalans, who had been granted it after Roger of Chirk's imprisonment in 1322. He also took Narberth from his cousin. In Haverford, he claimed not just his uncle's one-third share, but also the other two-thirds which had fallen into the control of the Crown. In this case, though, he then granted the whole to Queen Isabella, who kept it until her death, when it passed to her grandson, the Black Prince, the eldest son of Edward III. After the death of the Black Prince, it passed to his son, Richard, and on his coronation it thus merged with the Crown.

Locations on the inner tour illustrate how some of this wealth was spent. Mention has already been made of the rebuilding of St Mary's Church, Pembridge and the new chapel of St Peter's at Ludlow Castle. Roger also made provision for a new chantry (Mortimer's chapel) at St Mary Magdalene Church, Leintwardine (though it may not have been built until 1352–3). In December 1328, he granted lands and rent for nine chantry priests at the church to sing Masses daily for the souls of King Edward III, Queen Philippa, Queen Isabella, Bishop Burghersh, himself, his wife Joan, his children and their ancestors. In the following year he added a further priest. It is intriguing that, in 1353, King Edward III twice visited Leintwardine, making an offering of 20s on one visit and laying a cloth of gold before the statue of the Virgin on the other.

The North Range of Ludlow Castle is considered one of the finest examples of the period in the country. The photograph shows the great hall in the middle with the chamber block and the Garderobe Tower built by Roger Mortimer (1287–1330) to the right

The church of St Mary Magdalene at Leintwardine, looking up the nave to the chancel. The Mortimer Chapel is to the left (north) of the chancel. (Photograph © Robert Anderson)

At Wigmore, despite now owning Ludlow Castle only eight miles down the road, Roger initiated extensive rebuilding to transform the ancestral home into a palatial residence, where he entertained the royal family at a 'round table', and probably paid for rebuilding parts of the church.

In addition to the new church of St Peter's in the outer bailey of Ludlow Castle, Roger oversaw an ambitious programme of further improvements to the already grand castle. He added a new tower called the Garderobe Tower, built backing onto and breaking through the curtain wall. The tower had a number of bedrooms, each with its own garderobe (toilet), a great luxury at the time. Although the castle already had a solar block providing private accommodation on one side of the Great Hall, Roger built another set of private accommodation on the other side, the Great Chamber Block.

Roger's marriage to Joan, taking place as it did when the two were young teenagers, was a dynastic match organised by their families. Nevertheless, all the evidence is that Roger and Joan had a good relationship, not least in that she, unusually, accompanied Roger on his journeys around his estates in England and to Ireland. But when Roger was imprisoned in 1322, Joan and her daughters were also held in captivity. On his return from exile in 1326, he had become the lover of the queen and virtual ruler of the country. It is assumed that Roger was reunited with his wife at Pembridge in 1326. A far trickier problem was when he entertained the royal family at Ludlow Castle in 1329, which has given rise to a popular story which, almost certainly, never happened. Normal protocol would have been that the lady of the castle, in this case Joan, would give up the best rooms to the queen. As in this case the queen was also Roger's lover, this posed a delicate problem. The existence of two accommodation blocks either side of the Great Hall created a neat solution – Joan could remain in her own rooms, Queen Isabella and the royal party in the new block, whilst, diplomatically Roger slept with the soldiers! A great story, but it is both impractical and also there is no evidence that it happened in this way.

The great tournament and 'round table' that Roger organised at Wigmore in 1329, to celebrate the illustrious double wedding of two of his daughters, illustrates the grandeur that he was taking on. An event with Arthurian overtones was pretentious anyway, but Roger's behaviour scandalised people. He was accused of putting himself above the king, of wearing elaborate and rich clothes and expensive jewellery, and of sitting in the presence of the king. At Wigmore his own son declared Roger to be 'the King of Folly'.

ABOVE: Ludlow Castle seen from the top of the tower of St Laurence's Church

LEFT: A view of the ruined keep of Wigmore Castle, seen through the gatehouse

BELOW: The Garderobe Tower: an incredible construction built by Roger Mortimer, which breached the curtain wall, provided luxurious en-suite accommodation

Roger's pretensions, his alienation of other nobles, and perceived political mistakes (for example, the ambiguity of his role; a necessary but very unpopular peace treaty with Scotland; and the abrupt trial and execution of the king's uncle, the earl of Kent, for plotting to rescue his brother Edward II from captivity and restore him to the throne) led to growing opposition. As Edward III approached the age of 18, although still a minor, more and more he chafed under the control of Roger Mortimer, and his resentment grew such that he encouraged opposition to him. In October 1330, a group of young noblemen close to the king developed a plot to break into Nottingham Castle where Roger was staying. They succeeded in capturing him and he was taken straight to London, tried, condemned for treason for (amongst a long list of crimes) appropriating royal power, acting as if he was king, enriching himself and his family, and murdering Edward II. Roger Mortimer (1287–1330), first earl of March, was executed by hanging on 29 November 1330.

'King of Folly' (© Ethan Gould)

During the first part of his career everything indicates that Roger was a very capable military leader and administrator who maintained the Mortimer loyalty to the Crown. His personal life was settled with a strong marriage and many children and he was well placed to play a leading role in national affairs. But then circumstances pushed him into a course of action that spiralled out of control. Whilst we can assess events with the benefit of hindsight, it is important to remember that Roger, Isabella and their associates were caught up in the turmoil of new and unique events that had never happened before. There was no precedent for the forced abdication of a king and his replacement by his heir who was still a youth. Working it out as he went along and caught up in the turmoil of power and royalty, Roger inevitably made mistakes that led to his downfall.

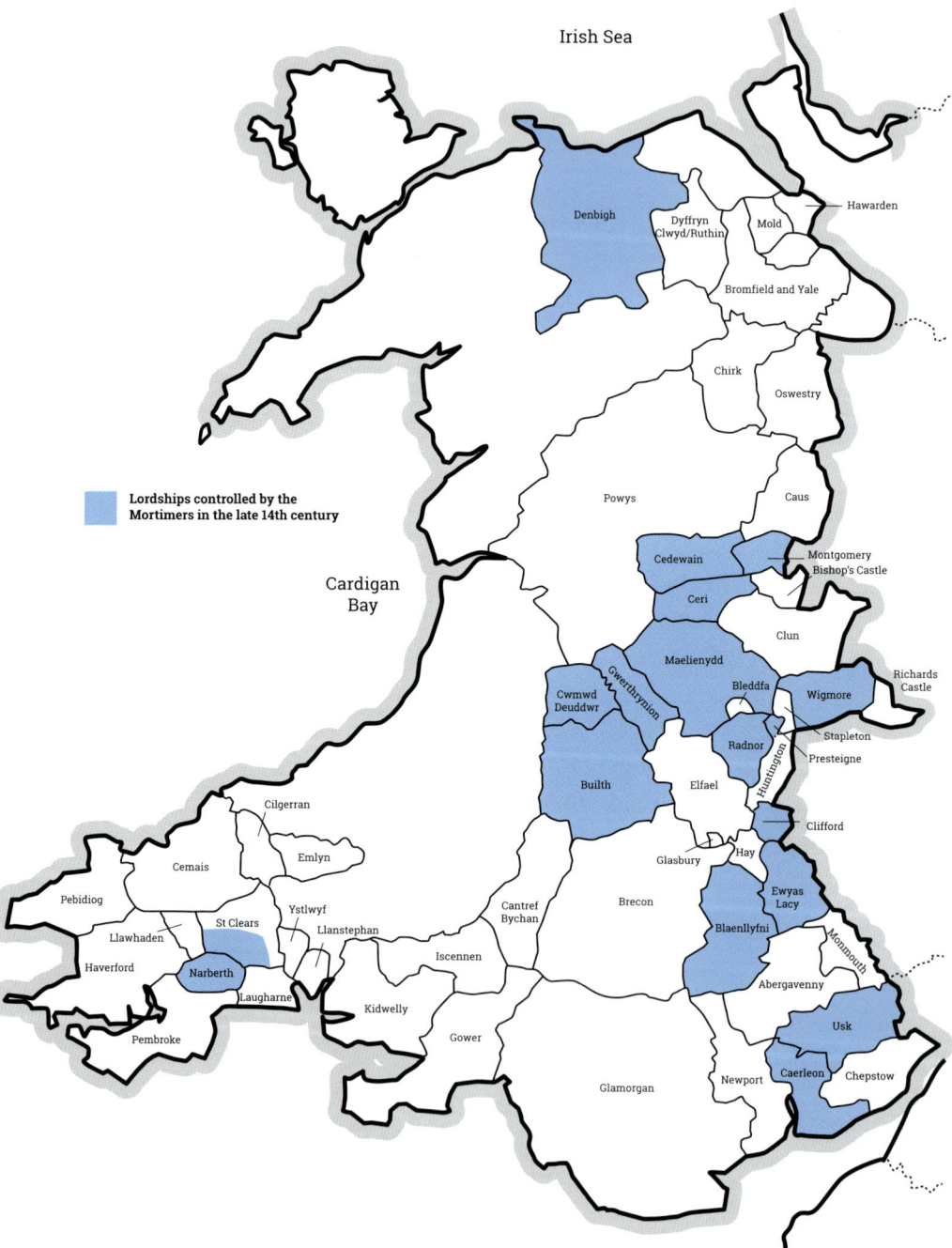

Map showing the Marcher lordships and the Principality of Wales in the third quarter of the fourteenth century, with those shaded being held by the Mortimers (© Jason Appleby)

FOUR

Recovery and a Claim to the Throne: 1330–1425

After the execution of Roger (1287–1330), the Mortimer family was not treated as harshly as they might have been. His grandson succeeded in recovering all the lands and titles, and married his own son into the royal family, gaining further lands in the Marches. However, a succession of early deaths and child heirs meant that the Mortimers were never in a position to have the impact on national affairs that matched their status. Instead, others used the Mortimer position as possible claimants to the Crown to rebel in their name. Increasingly, the Mortimers became pawns to be used by others. As noblemen of the highest status, they become less active in the area of this tour. The period covers five generations: Edmund Mortimer (d.1331); Roger Mortimer, 2nd earl of March (d.1360); Edmund Mortimer, 3rd earl of March (d.1381); Roger Mortimer, 4th earl of March (d.1398); Edmund Mortimer, 5th earl of March (d.1425).

The Mortimer family were not treated as harshly as they might have been in the aftermath of the execution of Roger (d.1330). This might suggest that the king knew that Roger had not had his father murdered and/or his appreciation that whilst there was a need to be rid of Roger, the family as a whole bore no blame. Roger's wife, Joan, was exempted from the confiscation of Roger's titles (the confiscation included the new earldom of March), property and estates. His son and heir, Edmund Mortimer (d.1331), was given back the family seat of Wigmore, together with Maelienydd and other Marcher lordships in 1331. However, Edmund's death just one year after his father's execution for treason threatened the whole Mortimer inheritance and the status of the family, for Edmund's son and heir was a child of only three.

FEMALE INHERITANCE, JOAN DE GENEVILLE, AND THE SYSTEM OF DOWER

Although inheritance in England was based on the principle of the eldest surviving son inheriting, if there was no male heir the inheritance was divided equally between surviving daughters. Consequently great family lordships that had been built up over a number of generations could disappear very quickly, for example the powerful de Braose, Marshal, and de Lacy families. The Mortimers not only avoided this fate through over 350 years of unbroken male succession, but even benefitted from it through their marriages to wealthy heiresses from those families.

Some families went to great lengths to avoid the inheritance being split by joint female inheritance. Joan de Geneville was the eldest granddaughter of Geoffrey de Geneville, who had married Maud, the heiress of the de Lacy estates which included Ludlow and lands in Ireland. Joan was born at Ludlow and when she was six her grandfather, whose own son had died, dispatched her two younger sisters to Aconbury Priory and settled all his lands on Joan.

Joan de Geneville married Roger Mortimer (d.1330) at Pembridge on 20 September 1301 when she was 15 and he was 14. As a result of her grandfather's actions, Joan was an heiress who brought large estates into the Mortimer family, and as Lady Mortimer, Lady of Ludlow, was a woman of important rank.

In 1308, aged 22 and herself a mother of four children, Joan became one of the chief ladies of the new queen's household. On 25 January in France, Edward II had married Isabella, the daughter of the King of France. On 7 February the 12-year-old bride arrived in England for the first time. When the royal party landed at Dover, Joan was among the ladies who greeted her and escorted her to London for the coronation of the new king and queen. It is not known whether Joan had a formal role in the coronation, but Roger was one of the lords who carried the royal robes in the procession.

During the first 20 years of her marriage to Roger, Joan was mother to 12 children who are known to have survived into adulthood. The consistent pregnancies are a strong indication that she must have regularly travelled with Roger between their estates and to attend on the king and Parliament. It is known that she travelled at least twice to Ireland with Roger, including his first visit in 1308 to claim their estates which included Joan's inheritance of Trim in Meath. She returned with him in 1310 when Ireland had more potential for danger. This suggests both a good personal relationship and involvement in the management of their estates.

The inventory of Joan's possessions (see p. 42) indicates a style of life fitting for the lady of one of the leading lords in the country. The existence of the inventory also illustrates how this apparently happy period of her life came to an abrupt end: Joan was not spared following Roger's capture in 1322 and subsequent imprisonment, escape and exile. She also was stripped of all her lands and possessions and was imprisoned first under house arrest in Hampshire, then, following Roger's escape, in Skipton Castle in Yorkshire. Whilst Joan was in custody in Hampshire, Queen Isabella, when writing to plead for better conditions for her, described Joan as 'our dear and well-beloved cousin'.

When Roger returned in 1326 everything was changed for Joan – they had been apart for over five years, her husband was the most important person in the kingdom and was the lover of the queen. Joan appears to have behaved with great dignity, re-establishing her household at Ludlow Castle and focusing on her role as Lady of Ludlow, even when Roger and Isabella visited with the young king Edward III. When Roger was elevated to the earldom of March, Joan became countess and she was included in all his endowments and attended the marriages of their children.

After Roger's fall and execution in 1330, Joan did not receive similar treatment to that meted out eight years earlier. Indeed, although Roger's lands and titles were confiscated, the king gave orders that Joan's wardrobe, jewels and other effects at Ludlow were not to be interfered with by those confiscating Roger's treasure. Shortly after, she was confirmed in possession of her own property, including Ludlow Castle from where she ran her estates, which included Orleton and Pembridge, until her own death in 1356. Two years before that, her grandson, Roger (d.1360) had regained the earldom of March, so Joan lived her last years as Dowager Countess of March.

Joan lived for 26 years after the death of her husband. When her own son died the following year there were three Mortimer widows alive: her mother-in-law Margaret de Fiennes (widow of Edmund Mortimer [1254–1304] from 1304–34), who survived both her son (Roger, d.1330) and grandson (Edmund, d.1331); Joan herself (widow of Roger [1287–1330] from 1330–56);

and Elizabeth de Badlesmere (widow of Edmund [d.1331] from 1331–56). This could have enormously complicated the management of estates.

Widows of tenants-in-chief were entitled to a proportion of their husband's estates – the dower, defined in the 1217 Magna Carta as a third of all the land that the husband held at the time of marriage and acquired during the course of it. Widows, therefore, could be rich and influential, particularly if they had an inheritance to add to their marriage portion and dower. Inevitably, King John (and to some degree earlier kings) had exploited this by forcing widows into a further marriage or exacting huge fines from them for the privilege of remaining single. Magna Carta tried to ensure that they could enter into their own inheritance, their marriage portion and their dower without difficulty and without charge, and established that a widow could not be forced into a further marriage.

During their husband's lifetime, the lady was responsible for running the household and was second-in-command after the lord. As widows, each of the above three ladies was responsible for running and administering large parts of the Mortimer estates and as such were independent and powerful women. Margaret held as her dower Knighton, Norton, Presteigne, Gwerthrynion and Radnor. Joan held Ceri, Cedewain and manors such as Orleton and Pembridge as her dower, Ewyas Lacy and Ludlow as her own inheritance. Elizabeth held Maelienydd and Cwmwd Deuddwr as her dower.

Only Elizabeth remarried, which was a further complication as the dower lands only reverted to the original family on the death of the second husband.

Edmund's death and the events of the next century provide a contrast with the first *c.*280 years of the family's history. Not only did the male succession continue unbroken in these earlier years but most were adults when they inherited (and the two who were not were in their mid-teens). Also, many survived into mid to late age, allowing them to use accumulated experience, wisdom and strength to expand the family's influence and wealth. With the death of Edmund Mortimer in 1331 there is a stark change in this run of luck – for the next nearly 100 years the Mortimer heirs inherited as very young children (successively, aged 3, 8, 7 and 7), and died whilst still young men (successively, aged 32, 29, 24 and 34).

This contributes to an intriguing irony: Edmund's son, Roger Mortimer (d.1360), succeeded in restoring almost the entirety of the family's estates, property and titles (and in doing so became, in 1354, the 2nd earl of March). As a consequence, the Mortimers resumed their place in the first rank of the nobility. Moreover, when Roger arranged the marriage of his son to a granddaughter of King Edward III, this put the Mortimers very close to the succession to the Crown of England. However, the repetition of long minorities and early deaths arguably meant that none developed the experience and maturity to take on a major role in national affairs matching their significant status. Further, their closeness to the royal succession put them in a position to be used as pawns by others in the dynastic struggles for power and influence.

As the young Roger Mortimer (1329–60) grew up he was gradually allowed to assume his inheritance from his father, gaining the family seat at Wigmore when he was 14 and further estates on the Welsh Marches two years later.

It was through the traditional Mortimer prowess in war that Roger proved himself invaluable, providing loyal service to King Edward III and his son, Prince Edward, known as the Black Prince. When still only 15 years old, Roger distinguished himself in a great tournament at Hereford. Three years later he participated in Edward III's wars in France, was knighted by the Black Prince and fought at the great Battle of Crécy. 'For his laudable service' he was given full control of his lands at Wigmore and the Welsh Marches.

Roger's military skill and loyal service brought him closer to the king and his son. In 1348, still only aged 20, he was honoured by being selected as one of the founding members of the king's new 'Order of the Garter'. He became an increasingly important commander and ally of the Black Prince.

With the support of the king (and following Edward III's two visits in 1353 to pray at and give gifts to the church of St Mary Magdalene in Leintwardine), the judgement on his grandfather was annulled in Parliament in 1354. The Mortimer claim to the title of earl of March was re-established and also their claim to all the estates amassed by the previous generations. This included most of the Marcher lordships newly acquired by his grandfather – Denbigh, Montgomery, Builth, Clifford, one-third of Ewyas Lacy, and Narberth. The king himself high-handedly dismissed any counter-claims to the lands (many of the estates had now been in the possession of other lords for 24 years), ensuring the complete rehabilitation of the Mortimer family.

The lordship of Denbigh is a good example of the upset that the Mortimer restoration created. After the execution of Roger in 1330, Denbigh had been given to William Montagu, later made earl of Salisbury (d.1344), who had been one of the group that captured Roger in Nottingham Castle. However, when the 2nd earl was able to reclaim Denbigh the Montagu family were ejected, much to their anger. Despite repeated petitions to the Crown, the Montagu family failed to reclaim Denbigh. Thus, it remained a Mortimer possession, passing to the House of York and then the Crown. In the south-west, Roger had to resort to court action to reclaim Narberth. One lordship that slipped from his grasp was Chirk, which had been given to the Fitzalans who were too powerful to be ejected. Consequently, Roger formally released all his rights in the castle of Chirk and the lands of Chirkland to the Fitzalans. Roger's service to the king and Black Prince continued to be recognised with further positions and income, and he was appointed a member of the king's council.

In 1358 Roger succeeded in uniting in his hands what had become the two separate lordships of Ludlow. It was earlier mentioned in the description of the Anarchy in the area that Joce de Dinan had become the lord of Ludlow, through his marriage to Sybil. Joce was then forced out of Ludlow by Gilbert de Lacy, the heir of another branch of the de Lacy family. In the middle of the thirteenth century, with no male heirs, the de Lacy inheritance was divided between two sisters, with Ludlow Castle and part of the town going to one (the de Geneville inheritance) and the rest of Ludlow to the other (the de Verdun inheritance) – the references are to the families that the sisters married into. An interesting quirk of this division was that, after some disputes, the two families agreed to take it in turns to nominate the clergy of St Laurence's, Ludlow. As recounted earlier, Roger Mortimer's marriage to Joan de Geneville added the de Geneville inheritance of Ludlow Castle and part of the town to the Mortimers' estates. Now his grandson, Roger (1329–60), agreed an exchange of lands with William de Ferrers who had inherited the de Verdun part, to bring the castle, manor and town of Ludlow back into a single lordship controlled by the Mortimers.

In 1360, at the age of 32, Roger died of a sudden illness on campaign in France, much to the distress of the king. His body was brought back to England and buried at Wigmore Abbey. The Wigmore Chronicle describes him as 'stout and strenuous in war, provident in counsel, and praiseworthy in his morals'. John Gour (a steward of the Mortimers whose effigy can be seen in St Mary's, Pembridge) was an executor of Roger Mortimer's will in 1360 and was appointed the keeper of the Mortimer estates in the Marches for the period of the minority of Edmund (1351–81).

Roger's early death meant that his son and heir Edmund Mortimer, 3rd earl of March and earl of Ulster (d.1381) was still a child of just eight years old. Two years before this, though, when Edmund was only six, Roger had used his favour with the royal family to arrange perhaps the greatest strategic marriage of the Mortimer history – in 1358 Edmund had been betrothed to Philippa, daughter, only child and heir of Edward III's second surviving son Lionel of Antwerp, duke of Clarence. The marriage between Edmund and Philippa took place in 1368. A few months after the marriage Lionel died, so at 16 years of age Edmund came into a great inheritance. As well as marrying into the royal family and their children entering the line of succession, Philippa brought to the Mortimers her mother's inheritance of Ulster and a large proportion of the Clare estates.

Thus, the lordship and castle of Usk passed to the Mortimers. Edmund and Philippa must have resided at Usk as their eldest son, Roger (4th earl of March, d.1398), was born in the castle. The Mortimers established an important first charter for the town of Usk and possibly built the circular Dovecote Tower and the Gatehouse in the outer curtain wall. The family became early patrons of the chronicler, Adam of Usk, who was born in the castle gatehouse. Thus, Edmund became the fourth largest landholder in England after the Crown, the Black Prince and the duke of Lancaster as well as the largest landowner in Ireland, and earl of Ulster as well as of March.

Aerial view of Usk Castle showing the outer gatehouse (top centre) and the circular Dovecote Tower (top right) possibly built by the Mortimers (© Paul R. Davis)

Part of the Gour effigy in Pembridge church, showing John Gour and his wife. John Gour was a local landowner and also worked for the Mortimers as a steward. He was an executor of the will of Roger Mortimer in 1360 and was the Keeper of the Mortimer estates in the Marches for the period of the minority of Edmund (1351–81). (Photograph © Robert Anderson)

Still only aged 19, Edmund was appointed Marshal of England in 1369 and served in campaigns in France and on diplomatic missions to France and Scotland. It appears that he benefitted from the support of his father's patron, the Black Prince.

As Edward III grew older and more senile, the last years of his reign saw increasingly bitter power struggles between different factions led by the Black Prince (the Prince of Wales) and his younger brother, John of Gaunt, duke of Lancaster, Edward's third son, who was effectively in charge of the government (the Black Prince being out of the country largely waging war in France).

The Mortimers' close association with the Black Prince put Edmund in that faction and, therefore, in opposition to John of Gaunt, who was already wary of the ambitions of the Mortimers (if the line of the Black Prince failed, Gaunt, as the next surviving son of the king, hoped that his family would inherit; however, the Mortimer descent from the second son, although through a daughter, was a threat). This started the enmity between the Mortimers and the house of Lancaster, which was to become, nearly 100 years later, the Wars of the Roses as rival claimants fought for the Crown.

The rivalry came to a head in 1376 when it became, for financial reasons, necessary to call Parliament. The Black Prince led the opposition to Gaunt in the House of Lords and Edmund led a group of nobles appointed to negotiate a joint approach with the House of Commons. In turn, the Commons appointed one Sir Peter de la Mere, who was a Mortimer steward and retainer, as their spokesperson in the negotiations, in so doing becoming the first Speaker of the Commons.

The Commons launched an attack on the corruption of officials and the wastage of public money – in effect an attack on John of Gaunt who was extremely unpopular. Everything changed, though, with the death of the Black Prince in June 1376, and Gaunt recovered ground. However, when Gaunt proposed a new law to restrict inheritance to the Crown to the male line only (in line with French practice, and eliminating any claim the Mortimers had) the Commons refused to discuss it. The Parliament set up a permanent council to be in constant attendance on the king with Edmund Mortimer as a member.

In June 1377, the aged King Edward III finally died, leaving his ten-year-old grandson, the son of the Black Prince, to become King Richard II. This brought the Mortimers even closer to the line of succession.

Edmund was prominent at the coronation. He became a member of the regency council, and led missions to Scotland as a negotiator and to inspect border defences.

In 1379, he was appointed as Lieutenant of Ireland, which was a prestigious role but which also, from Gaunt's perspective, removed him from the country. As the greatest Irish landowner and as earl of Ulster, he was very well suited for the position. He travelled to Ireland in May 1380 and operated with moderate success, but before he could achieve much he was taken ill and died in Ireland in December 1381. Edmund was buried at Wigmore Abbey, where he had granted lands to finance the costs of a major rebuilding programme.

Edmund's early death again left a child as his heir, this time aged seven. Roger Mortimer, 4th earl of March and 6th earl of Ulster (d.1398), inherited his parents' huge complex of estates in England, Wales and Ireland as well as, through his mother, a prominent place in the line of succession to the Crown.

As a wealthy child heir with a claim to the Crown, Roger was a strategic pawn in the struggles for power, influence and wealth. Eventually his guardianship and marriage were given to Richard II's half-brother, the earl of Kent, who paid £4,000 for the privilege. By about 1388, aged 14, Roger had married Kent's daughter, reinforcing his connections to the royal family.

His position as a possible heir to the childless Richard II influenced and circumscribed his life and short career. Although the story is probably untrue that Richard II publicly proclaimed Mortimer as his heir presumptive in Parliament in 1385, it is likely that in private Richard II for a period used the possibility of a Mortimer succession to curb the threats of his barons by pointing out that a possible heir was a mere child and, therefore, potentially worse than himself.

Roger came into full control of his estates in 1394, having undertaken a progress through his Welsh estates the year before, and began his short public career. Having been appointed in 1392 to the post of king's lieutenant in Ireland for the second time (the first time he was just seven years old!), he took up the post two years later when he and the king led a large force to Ireland. The force included a Mortimer contingent of 100 men-at-arms, two bannerets (a knight who led a company of troops during time of war under his own banner), eight knights, 200 mounted archers and 400 foot soldiers. Native Irish leaders had taken control over large parts of Ireland including the Mortimer estates in Meath, Ulster and Connacht. The relative claims, however, went largely unresolved and Roger spent much of his time in Ireland, which meant that his role in English political life was limited.

Despite this, his wealth and position made it inevitable that Roger would be caught up in the tensions, turmoil and opposition to the rule of Richard II and it appears that the king turned against him. In late 1397, whilst in Ireland, Roger was ordered to arrest his uncle Sir Thomas Mortimer, his father's illegitimate brother, who had headed the Mortimer Council during Roger's minority. If this was a test of his loyalty, Roger seems to have made little attempt to catch his uncle.

Along with other nobles, Roger was summoned in October 1397 to attend a Parliament called to meet at Shrewsbury. When Roger returned from Ireland for this, it is said that he was greeted by a crowd of 20,000 demonstrating their support by wearing hoods in the Mortimer colours and expecting him to lead the opposition to the arbitrary conduct of the king.

Roger though was careful to give no grounds for action against himself and managed to return to Ireland. However, he had still failed to hand over his uncle, and Sir Thomas Holland was sent across to arrest Roger for failing to carry out the king's command. Holland failed to fulfill his orders, only because shortly before his arrival Roger was killed in 1398 in a skirmish with the Irish. His badly mutilated body was eventually brought back for burial at Wigmore Abbey.

The death of Roger Mortimer possibly had more impact on national events than did his life. Although the king had turned against him and may well have been seeking his death, the killing of a possible heir to the throne could not go unpunished. So Richard II led another expedition to Ireland. This provided the opportunity for Henry Bolingbroke, son of John of Gaunt, to return from exile. With the king absent in Ireland and the Mortimer claim to the throne in abeyance as Roger's death had left another child heir aged only seven, Henry Bolingbroke was able to claim the throne, depose (and subsequently kill) Richard II, to be crowned Henry IV.

With Edmund Mortimer, 5th earl of March and 7th earl of Ulster (d.1425), inheriting at the age of seven, it meant that there was to be yet another long Mortimer minority. It is reasonable to say that his Mortimer inheritance, descent from Edward III and position in line to the succession to the Crown, wrecked his life. Just his existence was a potential threat and on a number of occasions others used his position as an excuse to rebel.

Henry IV, having seized the throne in dubious circumstances and with doubt about his legitimacy, was inevitably wary of other contenders, particularly the Mortimers. Accordingly, he placed his potential rival under strict supervision, and Edmund, with his younger brother Roger, lived as a royal ward, mostly at Windsor.

The first attempt to use Edmund's name to rebel was made by his own uncle, Sir Edmund Mortimer. Starting from a local dispute, there had been a growing rebellion, led by Owain Glyn Dŵr, to establish Welsh independence. In June 1402, when Owain led a force into mid Wales, Sir Edmund, as uncle of the young earl and head of the family, raised an army from Herefordshire and together with a contingent from Maelienydd marched to confront Owain. The armies met at Bryn Glas ('Green Hill'), Pilleth, with Owain's forces at the top

The site of the Battle of Pilleth or Bryn Glas. Pilleth church is the white building on the right. The Wellingtonias on the hillside on the left mark the site of where many of those killed were buried. As the bodies would not have been moved far unnecessarily, it is likely Edmund Mortimer was advancing up the hill on the left when the archers turned on his army

of the steep hill. Despite this disadvantage, Sir Edmund attacked and, when the men from Maelienydd changed sides, he was heavily defeated. Many English soldiers were killed and tradition states that the corpses were badly mutilated by the Welsh women. At this time border towns held by English lords, such as Knighton and Presteigne, were overrun and ransacked by the Welsh.

The battle at Pilleth, and its outcome, was a decisive event as the defeat of an English force gave credibility to Owain's rebellion. It also marked the decline of Mortimer military power – an example of the paradox that although now they were earls with a claim to the throne, their real power was much less significant.

Sir Edmund was captured, but the king forbade the payment of a ransom. Stuck in captivity, Sir Edmund switched sides and married one of Owain's daughters – an echo of his ancestor's marriage to the daughter of Llywelyn (Ralph and Gwladus Ddu). It is impossible to say whether the king, in not allowing the ransom to be paid, was justified in his suspicions of Sir Edmund's loyalty, or whether it was that which provoked him to rebel.

By the end of 1402 Sir Edmund was proclaiming that he and Owain would restore Richard II if he was still alive, or otherwise place his nephew, Edmund Mortimer (1391–1425) on the throne. Sir Edmund and Owain were joined by the duke of Northumberland and his son Henry Hotspur, who had their own dispute with Henry IV. Although Hotspur was defeated and killed at the Battle of Shrewsbury in 1403, Owain continued to cause trouble in Wales and the following year made an agreement with the King of France. By 1405, Sir Edmund had dropped the story that he was acting in the name of his nephew, the young earl, and announced a three-way agreement to split the country between himself, Owain and Northumberland.

In February 1405 the young earl and his brother were seized from their custody in Windsor Castle by Constance, Lady Despenser with the intention to take them to south Wales, but they were recaptured at Cheltenham, returned and put under closer guard. It seems that the intention was to unite them with their uncle, Sir Edmund, and Owain Glyn Dŵr. Later the same year in May, another revolt in Yorkshire publicised again the Mortimer claim to the throne.

Not surprisingly, more secure custody was recommended and in 1409 the brothers were placed in the care of Prince Henry.

When King Henry IV died in 1413, Edmund (1391–1425) was 22 and old enough to potentially pursue his own claim to the throne if he wished. Despite this, Henry V released him from custody and knighted him. In Parliament he was declared of age and allowed to inherit his lands. The new king's trust went only so far, however, and he kept Edmund in his company and made him pledge the huge sum of 10,000 marks (£6,666) for his loyalty.

The year 1415 became a notable one. Without seeking permission from the king, Edmund secured a dispensation from the Pope to marry someone within the prohibited degrees – all eligible women of a suitable rank were related to him in some way – and married Anne, the daughter of the earl of Stafford, also descended from Edward III. The king was not happy and imposed a large fine of 2,000 marks (£1,333) and also called in the 10,000 (£6,666) marks that had been pledged, which left Edmund with financial problems for the rest of his life.

A few months later, in July 1415, as the king was preparing to invade France, and having witnessed the king's will, Edmund found himself at the centre of the 'Southampton plot' to depose Henry and proclaim him king. The leader of the plot was Edmund's brother-in-law, Richard, earl of Cambridge and it is not clear whether Edmund had any involvement in it or just became aware of the plan. Whichever, he informed the king, who accepted his pledges of loyalty, pardoned him, and rewarded him by placing him on the commission that tried and condemned the plotters, including his brother-in-law, to death!

Towards the end of 1415, Edmund participated in the invasion of France, but was taken home with dysentery (which was very common) and so was not present at Agincourt. On his recovery he continued to serve on campaigns in France, and, after King Henry married in 1421, Edmund bore the queen's sceptre at her coronation.

When, in 1422, the king fell ill and died on campaign in France, leaving a baby son of only nine months old as his heir, it was a reversal of the circumstances 24 years before when Edmund's own youth meant that there was no viable Mortimer claim to the Crown. There is no evidence that Edmund tried to take advantage of this situation and he was appointed one of the baby king's councillors. Others though would continue to use his name and a distant kinsman, Sir John Mortimer, was accused of plotting a rising in Wales to make Edmund king (shortly afterwards Sir John was executed for attempting to escape custody in the tower). Rumour abounded and people such as the young king's uncle, the duke of Gloucester, used the size of Edmund's growing retinue to raise suspicions about his intentions.

Edmund still took an interest in the lives of people in the Wigmore/Ludlow area. He petitioned the bishop of Hereford to allow the burial of the dead at Orleton, as they had previously been buried at Eye church. The bishop tested the petition by sending two people to walk between Eye and Orleton. When they found that it was, indeed, very marshy and difficult to travel, he agreed to the petition.

Edmund was appointed, like his father and grandfather, to the post of Lieutenant of Ireland – probably to get him out of the country and away from the court – and travelled there in the autumn of 1424. He soon fell ill with the plague and died in January 1425 at his castle at Trim, becoming the third successive head of the family to die in Ireland.

It has been said that Edmund was a 'rudderless noble whose lineage placed him at the mercy of others'.

Edmund's brothers had died and he had no children, so the Mortimer inheritance (and all that went with it) passed through his sister Anne (the wife of the executed Richard, earl of Cambridge) to his nephew.

Orleton church with its graveyard, the latter due to the petitioning of Edmund Mortimer (photograph © Robert Anderson)

FIVE

A Mortimer Descendant Wins the Throne in Battle: 1425–85

In 1425 the Mortimer succession passed to Richard, the teenage son of Edmund's sister, Anne. Richard, whose parents both died when he was very young, had already inherited the dukedom of York so became not only the wealthiest subject in the kingdom but also someone with a good claim to the throne. Poor government and the infirmity of the king pushed Richard of York into armed opposition after decades of loyalty. This started the 30 years of civil war known as the Wars of the Roses. Ludlow Castle became one of his main homes and is where his sons were brought up. After defeat at the Rout of Ludford Bridge on the edge of Ludlow in 1459, Richard fled into exile. On his return he was killed in battle and his eldest son, Edward, took over leadership of the Yorkist cause. After victory at the Battle of Mortimers Cross in 1461, Edward was proclaimed king. In turn, he sent his eldest son, another Edward, to be brought up at Ludlow Castle under the guidance of 'the Prince's Council'. On the unexpected death of the king in 1483, the 13-year-old Prince Edward departed Ludlow for London, where he was fated to become one of the 'Princes in the Tower' who disappeared, presumed dead.

In 1425, Richard of York, although still only 14 years of age, had already had an eventful life: his mother, Anne Mortimer, had died when he was still a baby. In 1415, when only four years old, his father, Richard, earl of Cambridge had been executed for his plot (as recounted in the previous section) to depose King Henry V and put Edmund (Mortimer (1391–1425) on the throne. On the death of another uncle at Agincourt in the same year of 1415, he was recognised as the heir to the dukedom of York; then, in 1425, when Edmund Mortimer died without a son, he became, as the only son of Anne Mortimer,

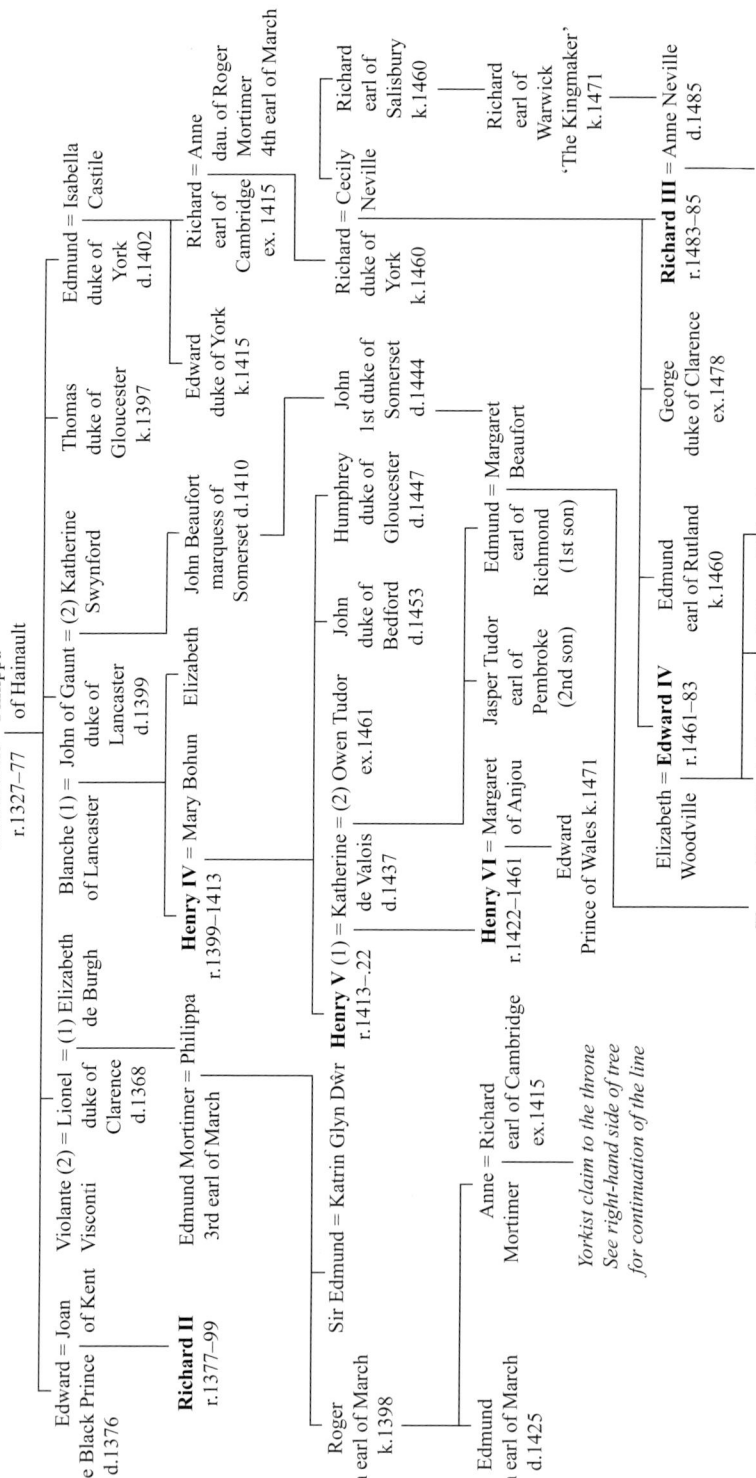

The Houses of York and Lancaster

heir to the vast and prestigious Mortimer inheritance. On his father's side he was a great-grandson of Edward III from that king's fourth surviving son, Edmund of Langley. In addition, as a Mortimer descendant he inherited their claim to the throne as a great grandson of Edward's second surviving son, Lionel, duke of Clarence. Some 35 years later, when circumstances put Richard of York and his son in a position to make an attempt for the Crown, it was on their Mortimer-Clarence descent that they most strongly based their claim.

In 1432, at the age of 21, Richard came into possession of all his estates as duke of York, earl of March, earl of Ulster and Lord Mortimer. As such, he was probably the wealthiest subject in the country, whilst also having a close relationship to the royal family.

With his lands and wealth spread across three countries, Duke Richard did not have a strong local affinity anywhere. However, his Mortimer inheritance in the Welsh Marches contributed a large part of his landed wealth and most of his soldiers. He came increasingly to use Ludlow Castle as one of his main bases, his family home, and the administrative centre of his Marcher estates. His sons, Edward (the future King Edward IV) and Edmund lived at Ludlow from 1452 when Edward was 10 and were brought up there. During the warfare that was to follow, Ludlow and the Marches were to be the centre of support for the Yorkist cause and the site of two significant conflicts.

The death in 1422 of Henry V had left his baby son, under a year old, as heir to the throne, resulting in an extremely long minority. As Henry VI became an adult it became increasingly clear that he was unsuited to rule, and was prone to periods of passivity and mental breakdown. As a result, the Lancastrian nobles jostled for power and influence to the detriment of the governance of the country. His household and court were a greedy, violent and corrupt faction; without a strong king, justice was often arbitrary and disputes settled by violence. Overseas, the lands gained in France by Henry V were gradually being lost.

Although the most important member of the royal family after the king and the greatest magnate in the country, it appears that for nearly 20 years Richard took no steps to exploit his position. He was a loyal servant of the Crown, despite the deteriorating situation at home and abroad, serving in positions such as lieutenant-general and governor of the kingdom of France and the king's lieutenant in Ireland. In 1447 Richard, with Henry VI still childless, became heir presumptive to the throne.

By 1450, the political situation in England was becoming more and more tense. Henry VI and his Lancastrian supporters were suspicious of Richard of York and kept him from his rightful place on the royal council. Increasingly, Richard was being seen by others as an alternative to the ruling regime around the king.

The first trouble was sparked in 1450 by a popular uprising of Kentish rebels which aimed to force the king to replace his Lancastrian councillors with Duke Richard. Richard returned from Ireland with the declared aim of reforming the government (not to seize the throne). This initiated a nine-year period of manoeuvring for position during which Richard started by, probably sincerely, claiming that his quarrel was with the king's councillors and not the king himself; but towards the end circumstances pushed him to complete opposition and to assert his 'greater right' to the Crown.

He clashed with the duke of Somerset who controlled the government and, in 1452, attempted to oust Somerset by force of arms. However, this failed when, confronted by a greatly superior army at Dartford, he was forced to submit. Within a year, though, the king had his first total mental collapse, which lasted 18 months, and Richard was officially appointed Protector. His position was weakened though when the queen, Margaret of Anjou, gave birth to a son and heir. When Henry VI recovered his wits there was no longer a need for a Protector.

By this time, Richard had allied himself with his powerful relations in the Neville family – his brother-in-law the earl of Salisbury and his nephew the earl of Warwick (later known as the Kingmaker).

In 1455 Richard and the Nevilles were summoned to face a Great Council at Leicester where they would probably have been arrested and charged with treason. Instead, they marched towards London and defeated and killed Somerset in the First Battle of St Albans, described as a murderous brawl in the streets as only 60 men were killed - the first skirmish in what became known as the Wars of the Roses between the Lancastrian branch of the royal family and the Yorkist claimants.

Having gained the upper hand, Richard again became Protector, but the queen remained implacably opposed to him and soon dismissed his government.

By 1459 the queen and her advisors decided that the time was right finally to crush the Yorkists. Richard and the Nevilles were pointedly excluded from a Great Council and rightly concluded that the intent was to condemn them for treason. Once again they mustered their forces. Richard and his sons were at

Ludlow where they were joined by the Nevilles before advancing to Worcester to petition the king. However, faced by a royal army of $c.12,000$ knights and soldiers, roughly twice the size of their army, the Yorkists fell back on their stronghold of Ludlow.

The king and royal army marched on Ludlow, passing through Leominster then Richards Castle towards Ludlow, where on 12 October 1459 the Yorkists set up their defences at Ludford just to the south of the Broad Gate entrance to Ludlow and across the Ludford Bridge crossing of the river. The actual presence of the king with a larger force, and the defection of some of the Yorkist troops to the king's side, led Richard and his commanders to conclude that their position was hopeless, and they decided to flee. The affair was known as the Rout of Ludford Bridge, because no battle was fought, but with the flight of the Yorkist leaders Ludlow was defenceless and it was savagely pillaged by the Lancastrian force. Richard, the Nevilles and their followers were declared traitors and stripped of all their lands and offices.

On fleeing, the York family separated, with Richard and his younger son, Edmund, seeking refuge in Ireland, and Edward, Salisbury and Warwick going to Calais. The family splitting to different places may have been to reduce risk or could indicate that Edward was now disillusioned with his father, who had failed to defend his heartlands in the Marches and was, anyway, distrusted by his peers. Effective leadership of the Yorkist cause had passed to the cousins Warwick and Edward, who had been granted the earldom of March by his father in 1445.

In June 1460, Salisbury, Warwick and Edward returned, entered London peacefully before going on to attempt to meet with the king at Northampton. When their peaceful overtures were refused and they were denied access to the king, armed conflict followed which was easily won by the Yorkists. The king was taken unharmed and, only nine months after the disaster at Ludford Bridge, a Yorkist government was set up under an obedient king.

Richard of York didn't return to the country until September 1460. Whilst at Ludlow his lords and followers urged him to take the throne, asserting the Mortimer descent from Lionel of Clarence. Richard progressed to London where, to the embarrassment of Warwick, Salisbury and his own son, Edward, he indeed demanded the throne. He had no support from the other peers of the realm and Parliament arranged a compromise, the Act of Accord, under which Richard would inherit on the death of the king, thus disinheriting the king's son. Not surprisingly, Henry's queen refused to accept this arrangement.

Richard, duke of York and his son as Edward IV, depicted in stained glass in St Laurence's Church, Ludlow

The queen, Margaret of Anjou, duly fled to Wales with her son to set about raising an army there, before sailing to Scotland to raise another in the north. As Richard was now Protector again, technically the queen and her supporters were rebels. Rashly he decided to move against them, leaving Warwick in charge of the king and sending Edward, aged 18, to his first independent command in the Welsh Marches. Richard was lured into attacking the larger royal forces and on 30 December 1460, he was defeated and killed at the Battle of Wakefield, and most of his army slaughtered.

Meanwhile Edward (who would have heard within a couple of days of the death of his father) was at Ludlow and Wigmore expecting and waiting for the advance of the Lancastrian army from south Wales, which was bound to strike at the heart of the Yorkist/Mortimer strength.

As the Lancastrian army, led by Jasper Tudor, moved up from south Wales Edward set up his positions at Mortimers Cross at the southern edge of the Wigmore lordship.

THE BATTLE OF MORTIMERS CROSS

Perhaps learning from his father's mistakes at Ludford Bridge, Edward had carefully selected a site to defend Wigmore where he would not be boxed in with his back to a river and where he could use the ground to his advantage. The site at Mortimers Cross (almost certainly called this as a Mortimer had erected a cross there – the current crossroads didn't exist then – probably a little to the south of the current crossoads where the old Roman road, Hereford Lane, diverts away from the turnpike road going towards the village) also meant that his army could quickly move to Ludlow if that was the target of attack

There is very little known about the battle, partly because it happened so far from London where attention was focussed on the advance of the queen's royal army from the north following their victory at Wakefield, and partly because its significance only became clear afterwards. The results are awaited of a recent archaeological investigation to determine the exact site of the battle.

It is likely that Edward positioned his army across the old Roman road (the main north-south route), facing south with his flanks protected by the river Lugg on one side and steep forested hills on the other (in which he could also conceal his archers and guns). The possible site of his forces is indicated by two traditions – the stump of the once massive Battle Oak situated on the original crossroads and the cottage called Blue Mantle (see below).

The sign for the Mortimers Cross Inn, making a play on the parhelion with a white rose of York surrounded by rays of the sun on a flag as the central sun.

While Edward awaited the arrival of the Lancastrian army, there are indications that buildings such as the church at Aymestrey were used as stores and stables. Most of Edward's supporters were local people from north Herefordshire, including his godfather, Richard Croft, of nearby Croft Castle (his effigy remains in Croft church) and John Lingen, who was buried at Aymestrey church.

On 3 February, St Blaise's Day (the date is disputed, the alternative being 2 February, Candlemas, when a service is still held in the Volka chapel of Kingsland church to pray for the souls of those who died in the battle), the two armies met. Before the battle started people were aghast to see three suns shining in the sky (an atmospheric phenomenon now known as a parhelion, caused by ice crystals refracting light) and were much afraid. With great presence of mind, Edward reassured his army by proclaiming that the three suns signified the Father, the Son and the Holy Ghost. Afterwards, Edward was to incorporate the 'Sun in Splendour' into his emblem.

Before a medieval battle, heralds often passed between the armies to attempt a peaceful settlement. Although, after the slaughter of his father and his army at Wakefield, it is unlikely that Edward would have done this, there is a local tradition that his herald, who was called Blue Mantle, was treacherously slain and this is reflected in the cottage of this name by the Battle Oak.

Edward led his army to victory and the Battle of Mortimers Cross was followed by the now customary slaughter and blood-letting. Shortly after it was reported that 4,000 had died in the battle and subsequent rout. As was often the case, this was almost certainly an exaggeration. The armies probably numbered only 2–3,000 each. However, the tradition concerning the slaughter of the defeated Lancastrians is probably true as Edward will have wanted to avenge the sacking of Ludlow following Ludford Bridge and the slaughter at Wakefield.

Following the battle, Edward stayed for three weeks in Hereford, where the captured leaders of the Lancastrians were executed, including Jasper Tudor's father Owen (grandfather of Henry Tudor

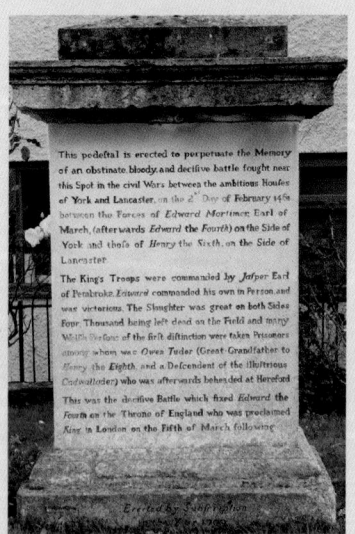

Monument to the battle, erected in 1799 on the edge of Kingsland

> who was to become King Henry VII 24 years later). Edward then marched on London where he was proclaimed king by the Londoners as Edward IV.
>
> One mile to the south of Mortimers Cross, a monument was erected in 1799 to commemorate the battle, which can be seen in the fork of the road on the access lane to Kingsland from the A4110.
>
> Edward IV founded two chantry chapels in Kingsland church, one for 'Our Lady' and the other for 'St Katherine' to 'pray for the souls of those slain in the battle of Mortimers Cross'.

Although, following his victory at Mortimers Cross, Edward was proclaimed king by Londoners on 4 March, his position was not secure. Margaret of Anjou had marched south after the Battle of Wakefield and defeated Warwick at the Second Battle of St Albans on 17 February. Although Margaret had managed to release Henry VI from Warwick's hands during the battle, her support had begun to drift away and with London against her she retreated north. Edward followed and on 29 March defeated with great slaughter the Lancastrian army at Towton, where about 50,000 men are believed to have fought for six hours in the snow.

Edward, grandson of Anne Mortimer, earl of March, earl of Ulster and lord of Ludlow was formally crowned king on 28 June 1461, and all the Mortimer lands and titles passed to the Crown.

Edward IV maintained his connection with Ludlow, spending a week there in September 1461, and in December granted the town a new charter. He personally contributed to further rebuilding of St Laurence's, making it one of the largest parish churches in England and Wales. He sent his eldest son and heir (another Edward, at the young age of three) to Ludlow in 1473 to be brought up and educated with his own household away from the intrigues of London. Whilst still a baby, the rule of the prince's household and lands (which included the Principality of Wales and later the lands of the earldom of March) had been entrusted to a council. 'The Prince's Council' accompanied the three-year-old prince to Ludlow together with a number of royal servants. From 1476 the Prince's Council developed into the main agent of royal authority in Wales and the Marches.

Ludlow Castle was Prince Edward's principal home for ten years. He was resident there when, aged 13, his father, King Edward IV, suddenly died in April 1483. The prince left Ludlow to travel to London to be acclaimed king, but on the way was intercepted by his uncle, Richard of Gloucester, who was afraid of the prince coming under the influence of his mother's extensive Woodville family. This set in train the events that led to the coronation of his uncle as Richard III, Prince Edward's confinement with his brother Richard in the Tower of London and their subsequent disappearance, leading to their sobriquet 'the Princes in the Tower'.

As recounted on p. 43 the death or survival of King Edward II (and the possible involvement of Roger Mortimer) is shrouded in mystery. Equally, mystery

Edward, Prince of Wales – the future Edward V – depicted in stained glass in St Laurence's Church, Ludlow

surrounds the death of the 'Princes in the Tower'. At the time, it was assumed that they had been murdered, and blame was attached to their uncle, Richard III, who was subsequently vilified by Tudor propagandists, including Shakespeare. Today, historians are divided, with many arguing that others had greater motive to see them dead.

The Yorkist dynasty, which had based its claim to the Crown on its Mortimer inheritance, came to an end in 1485, when Richard III was defeated at the Battle of Bosworth and Henry Tudor became King Henry VII.

The Mortimer story, though, does not finish there – for to unite the warring factions, King Henry married Elizabeth, the eldest daughter of Edward IV, which means that all subsequent monarchs are descended from the Mortimers.

Postscript: Ludlow, Capital of the Marches

As we have seen, this tour shows the extent to which places such as Ludlow, Wigmore, Montgomery, Denbigh, Usk, Haverford and the surrounding towns and villages were, for over 400 years, centres of major events, and home to great lords, future kings and their families.

With the changing times (for example, the impact on local communities as castles became obsolete when gunpowder and new technology made their defences redundant and other places were more comfortable to live in); and the absorption of the Mortimer inheritance into the Crown, many of the places on this tour, such as Richards Castle, Pembridge, Ewyas Lacy, Clifford, Usk and even Wigmore, had already begun a slow decline into rural tranquillity.

Richards Castle is often cited as one of the most interesting examples of a failed borough in the Marches. In 1304 it was recorded that over 100 burgesses lived there, and the outlines of the earthworks of the borough are still evident. Once there was no point in maintaining the castle, however, the town was in the wrong place – the location on an inaccessible hill with views of the surrounding countryside was good for military purposes, but not appropriate for a trading town – and so declined, particularly as neighbouring Ludlow was much better situated on major route-ways for trade. Eventually, a new village of the same name was established down in the valley on the road between Leominster and Ludlow.

In contrast, the royal connection with Ludlow continued when Henry VII granted to his eldest son, Prince Arthur, the castle, town and lordship of Ludlow, and sent him there with a Council. Following his marriage to Catherine of Aragon, Arthur died in 1502 aged 16 at Ludlow Castle, and his heart was interred at St Laurence's Church whilst his body was taken to Worcester Cathedral for burial. The king allowed the Council to remain at Ludlow until Prince Henry (later King Henry VIII) arrived as the new Prince of Wales.

Although it had not been a Marcher lordship, for two centuries Ludlow was the home of the Council in the Marches of Wales – in effect the capital of Wales and the border regions. Although Ludlow Castle was only used as a royal residence once more – by the Princess Mary (later 'Bloody' Queen Mary I) and her court in the three winters between 1525–28 – its use by the President and members of the Council, its lawyers and administrators, brought wealth and influence to Ludlow. This provided a market for local tradespeople, which combined with the wealth from the local wool and cloth trades to generate a high level of economic prosperity for the town.

The influence and power of the Council declined in the second half of the seventeenth century and it was abolished in July 1689 following a decision to centralise power in London.

The tower of St Laurence's Church dominates the Ludlow skyline

Inner Mortimer Tour

A summary of Mortimer connections and remains in each location

1) Wigmore

Location

The village of Wigmore is centred on the junction of the A4110 and the unclassified road to Ludlow. The church of St James is on a ridge overlooking the village along a lane/footpath just to the west of the A4110 opposite the junction. The ruins of Wigmore Castle are accessed via a footpath that continues north-west from the church and lane. Please note that there is no vehicular access to the castle and no parking at the church: please park in the Village Hall car park (a short way along the Ludlow road) and walk from there. Wigmore Abbey is located along an unclassified road signposted to Burrington and Downton, that turns eastwards off the A4110 about one mile north-west of Wigmore and just south of Adforton. Note that the remains of Wigmore Abbey are privately owned and in part incorporated into the current house; there is no public access to the site but aspects can be seen from the lane and from a footpath on the eastern side.

Mortimer Connections

Wigmore is both the starting point of, and also the focal point for, much of the history of the Mortimers in the Welsh Marches and England. The first castle at Wigmore had been built by William fitz Osbern, earl of Hereford, between 1068 and 1071. When William's son, Roger, rebelled against the king in 1075, his lands and castles were taken from him. Wigmore was given to Ralph Mortimer (d.1115–27) and it became the chief centre of his lands in England, held directly from the king as a tenant-in-chief. It is one of the few Herefordshire boroughs mentioned in Domesday. Successive Mortimers over two and a half centuries (particularly, Roger [d.1282] in the mid thirteenth century and Roger [d.1330] in the 1320s) rebuilt the castle, enlarging it, strengthening its fortifications and improving the living arrangements.

For over 200 years it was a fortress around which wars were fought, and it was besieged on several occasions. A few highlights from the main text illustrate this: during the civil wars of King Stephen's reign Wigmore was the focal point of support for the king in the central Marches, becoming increasingly isolated and indeed under siege in 1149. A few years later in 1155, when Hugh Mortimer (d.1181–85) refused to surrender Bridgnorth Castle to Henry II, the king's forces besieged and took Wigmore. Just over 100 years later in February 1264 the supporters of Simon de Montfort combined with the Welsh to besiege Wigmore. Later the same summer, Wigmore was under attack again by de Montfort's forces and this time was captured. When de Montfort was killed in 1265 at the Battle of Evesham, Roger Mortimer (d.1282) sent his severed head to Wigmore Castle as a trophy for his wife – an indication of the deep and bitter hatred that had been generated.

The final conquest of Wales at the end of the thirteenth century, combined with the increasing wealth and status of the Mortimers, meant that Roger Mortimer (d.1330) could transform the existing fortress into a palatial residence which was the equal of Ludlow in splendour. As the ancestral home and centre of their estates, Wigmore would always have been a place that was home and where the Mortimers entertained lords, kings and queens at great feasts and tournaments, such as the one that Roger held in 1329 when his son declared him to be the 'King of Folly' for his pretentious behaviour.

The results of archaeological excavations between 1996 and 1998 shed light on life at Wigmore Castle – as a comfortable residence (in the fourteenth century most of the windows were glazed, the walls had decorative plaster and the floors were laid with glazed tiles embellished with Mortimer motifs); as a military fort (arrowheads and bits of armour); on aspects of everyday life (including pottery from both the local area and overseas); on their diet (which at times contained oysters, deer and hazelnuts; and on pest control (the bones of cats that would have controlled rats and mice).

The indications are that during the fourteenth century Wigmore retained an importance as the ancestral home, with a dual role alongside Ludlow, which the family had acquired in 1308. However, after the Mortimer inheritance passed first, in 1425, to the duke of York and then, through his son Edward IV, to the Crown, Ludlow was the preferred residence and Wigmore declined fairly quickly. By the 1530s Wigmore Castle was described as 'utterly decayed in lodging'. In 1601 the castle was purchased by Thomas Harley of Brampton Bryan. The Parliamentarian Harleys were unable to defend both Wigmore and their castle at Brampton Bryan during the Civil War and Lady Brilliana Harley ordered Wigmore to be partly razed.

A borough had developed near the castle but, as its economy would have been strongly linked to trade and services with the castle, it too declined with the castle.

The parish church of St James was built, maintained and extended under the patronage of the Mortimers. It was probably first built towards the end of the eleventh century, as from 1086 Ralph Mortimer (d.1115–27) started to give pieces of land to the parish church and in 1100 endowed it as a small college of three canons, presumably superseded by Wigmore Abbey. It appears that Roger Mortimer (d.1330) supported extensive building work when the chancel was rebuilt and a south aisle added.

Pages 9, 11 and 15 recount the removal of the Augustinian canons from their first priory at Shobdon to their final settlement by Hugh Mortimer (d.1181–85) at Wigmore Abbey, which was dedicated in 1179. The abbey became a place of spiritual significance to the family as nearly all the Mortimer lords were buried there. Indeed, the inventories of Roger and Joan's possessions in 1322 show that Joan was probably living at the abbey whilst the castle was being rebuilt (see p. 30). Wigmore Abbey continued until 1538 when it was closed during the programme of dissolution of monastic foundations under Henry VIII.

What to see
One of the most significant castles in Britain, Wigmore Castle is now best described as impressive romantic ruins. The site is privately owned but in the care of English Heritage and there is free access across the site. In 1996 English Heritage undertook a two-year campaign of repair and excavation. This was the first time that a 'soft capping' approach was adopted to deliberately retain a site's wildness and protect its rare flora and fauna. There are spectacular views of the Wigmore glacial plain from the keep. Much of the ruins are buried under centuries of accumulated soil and crumbled stonework. Still visible are the remains of the bailey curtain walls including several towers and a gatehouse; traces of buildings in the bailey; and the buildings and shell keep on the motte. Access to the site is through the gatehouse, though the lower part is buried under accumulated debris and soil so you enter through what would

Wigmore Castle in moonlight. Perhaps it was on such a night that Maud de Braose, wife of Roger Mortimer, received her grisly trophy – the severed head of Simon de Montfort

have been the upper part of the archway. You can wander round the site and climb up to the keep, imagining the past splendour of the castle as it stands above the surrounding countryside; the bustle of everyday life, and the threat of warfare, siege and capture.

The parish church of St James. Herringbone masonry can be seen on the external north wall and is thought to date to *c.*1050 when this formed part of an earlier Saxon church. It has recently been uncovered in the interior of the church. Most of the building dates from the Mortimer period, with parts from across the centuries, including the nave (which was of exceptional height and width), the chancel, which was rebuilt in the early fourteenth century when the south aisle and its roof were added – possibly funded by Roger (d.1330) – and the tower, which dates from the mid fourteenth century.

Wigmore Abbey. There is no public access to the site but there are surviving fragments of the twelfth-century walls, fourteenth-century abbot's lodging and other buildings, parts of which are incorporated into a private house and which can be glimpsed from the lane, and a footpath on the south side of the lane, a few hundred metres past the abbey site.

LEFT: Masonry from the south wall of the transept of Wigmore Abbey. RIGHT: The gatehouse that adjoins the fourteenth-century Abbot's Lodging can be seen from the lane to the north

2) Richards Castle

Location
Although the current village of Richards Castle is in the valley bottom on the B4361, the original settlement was half a mile up the hill to the west. Turn off the B4361 by the Castle pub on the unclassified road signposted to the Historic Church. Go past a number of black-and-white timbered houses and farms and park on the triangular village green (the medieval market area) on the left where the castle and church are signposted. The castle is accessed through the church grounds and graveyard.

Mortimer connections
The castle was first built in about 1050, one of only four castles built before the Conquest, by Richard fitz Scrob and held by his descendants. During the anarchy and civil wars of 1138–54 the strongholds of Richards Castle (owned by Osbern fitz Hugh) and Wigmore (Hugh Mortimer, d.1181–85) were allied in their support for King Stephen and became increasingly isolated, particularly when the lords of Ludlow and Kingsland switched sides.

Through marriage, Richards Castle came into the possession of Robert Mortimer from Essex in 1210 and remained in the possession of his descendants until 1304. There has been no evidence of a family relationship between the two Mortimer families of Wigmore and Richards Castle, however, recent research by Dr Ian Mortimer has discovered that there is indeed a relationship. The military alliances continued and the Mortimers of Richards Castle supported the Mortimers of Wigmore in their wars in Wales and disputes with Simon de Montfort. (There is more information in the insert box on p. 5.)

What to see
There is open access to the castle, and you can walk around the remains of the wall and tumbled-down keep. Its significance here is that it is the site of one of the oldest motte and bailey castles in the country. Next to the castle is the church of St Bartholomew, founded in the twelfth century. This has a separate late thirteenth-century bell tower. Inside the church, at the north end of the Chapel of St John, is a large recess, probably constructed for the tomb of the chapel's founder, Hugh Mortimer, though there are no signs that it was ever actually used. The church, open daily, is now in the care of the Churches Conservation Trust though it is still used for burials and two services a year.

TOP LEFT: The detached bell tower at Richards Castle, the siting of which, and its lack of windows in the wall facing the castle, indicate it was built with the defence of the castle in mind.
TOP RIGHT: Remains of castle walls at Richards Castle. Only four castles were built before the Norman Conquest in 1066, with this one begun by Richard fitz Scrob in about 1050. Only the motte and earthworks of the bailey enclosure remain of the original castle. The stone-built castle dates from c.1175, and some ruins of the large octagonal stone tower, the gatehouse, sections of a wall and towers (one built by the Mortimers of Richards Castle) are visible.
BELOW: St Bartholomew's Church, Richards Castle. The south aisle (to the right of the picture) was built between 1310 and 1320 and contained the chantry of St Mary the Virgin, built by Joan Mortimer who, with her sister, had inherited Richards Castle in 1304

In 1216 King John granted Robert Mortimer a charter for a fair and market, and by 1300 Richards Castle was a small town. By 1400, it had shrunk to two farms and a few cottages and (as explained on p. 61) is often regarded as one of the most interesting examples in the Marches of a failed borough.

3) ORLETON

Location
To find Orleton turn off the B4361 onto the B4362. Take the first right into the village, go past the school and the church is on the left.

Mortimer connections
The manor of Orleton had belonged to Queen Edith, the widow of King Edward the Confessor. On her death in 1075, the manor was given to Ralph Mortimer (d.1115–27) and remained in the possession of the Mortimers.

The parish church of St George was first built under Mortimer patronage in the twelfth century, with substantial rebuilding and enlarging in the thirteenth/ fourteenth centuries, including the intriguing stone carved heads.

Orleton formed part of the estates of Joan de Geneville following the death of her husband, Roger (d.1330).

Edmund Mortimer, shortly before his death in 1425, petitioned the bishop of Hereford to bury the dead at Orleton, as they had previously been buried at Eye church. The bishop tested the petition by sending two people to walk between Eye and Orleton. When they found that it was, indeed, very marshy and difficult to travel, he agreed to the petition.

The carved dragon in Orleton church

What to see
Much of the parish church of St George was built during the Mortimer period – the nave dating from the twelfth century, the chancel from the thirteenth, the chancel arch *c.*1330s, and the tower from the mid fourteenth century.

Of particular interest is the twelfth-century font, which is carved with several arched bays with a standing figure of an Apostle under each arch (only St Peter is identifiable by his key), and also the carved dragon, both of which are characteristic of the Herefordshire School of Romanesque Sculptors (see pp. 10–12). There are two remarkable wooden chests, both made from oak; stylistic evidence suggests the smaller chest is thirteenth century, whilst the larger one has been dated by dendrochronology to mid-fourteenth century.

The stories and traditions associated with the six stone carved heads placed either side of and around the chancel arch and their associations with kings, queens, lords and bishops are described in detail on pp. 44–45.

4) Yarpole

Location
It is worth making a short detour into the village of Yarpole (turn off the B4362 opposite the entrance to Croft Castle).

Mortimer connections
Yarpole was part of the lordship of Richards Castle, thus owned in the thirteenth century by the Mortimers of Richards Castle.

What to see
The main interest is St Leonard's Church, which has the second detached bell tower on the tour. The construction of the original

The detached bell tower at Yarpole church

wooden framework has been dated (by dendrochronology) to 1196, from timber that was growing in the 990s. The lower part of the tower was later encased in stone. The earliest surviving fabric of St Leonard's Church, which is also worth a visit, dates to the early 1300s. Nowadays, it has been sympathetically refurbished to be a hub of community life in the village, incorporating the village shop/post-office and a café as well as continuing as the parish church. Both church and bell tower are open daily with informative guidebooks. The bell tower has an audio commentary and information panels.

5) CROFT

Location

Opposite the turning to Yarpole off the B4362 there is a turning for Croft Castle. Take this and follow the road through the gate and into the lands of the estate, now in the care of the National Trust. Keep going till you come to a car park on the right-hand side, shortly before a mock castle entrance to a driveway. Walk down the driveway to the church, which is to the left of Croft Castle itself. (Please note: if intending to visit the house or the gardens, you need to acquire a ticket.)

Mortimer connections

The Croft family, who have lived at Croft Castle since the eleventh century (with an interruption between 1746–1923), were neighbours and allies of the Mortimers. There is a tradition that a Croft was active with the Mortimers in the escape of Lord Edward from Hereford in 1265. Sir Richard Croft was a key local supporter of Richard, duke of York and fought with his son, Edward, at the Battle of Mortimers Cross. Sir Richard was a close confidant of Edward when he became king, and his wife, Eleanor, was a governess of the king's sons.

What to see

The current Croft Castle, which is now owned by the National Trust (admission charges for non-members), mainly dates from the fifteenth and sixteenth centuries. The castle is set in extensive gardens, parkland and woodland with many walks, including one up to the Iron Age fort of Croft Ambrey. The early fourteenth-century church of St Michael contains the magnificent tomb and effigies of Sir Richard Croft and his wife Eleanor.

The effigy and tomb of Sir Richard Croft, who fought at the Battle of Mortimers Cross (photographs © Logaston Press)

6) Mortimers Cross/ Aymestrey

Location

Mortimers Cross is at the crossroads formed by the A4110 and the B4362. Aymestrey is a short way north up the A4110.

Mortimer connections

It is assumed that the name Mortimers Cross comes from a cross erected by one of the Mortimers. The current crossroads did not exist at the date of the battle, when the junction would have been a little further south where the Roman Road (now Hereford Lane) bears to the right from the turnpike road going towards Kingsland. Battle Oak was situated on this junction.

The boxed information on pp. 73–75 describes the events leading up to the Battle of Mortimers Cross, the battle itself and the aftermath when a Mortimer descendant claimed the throne to become Edward IV.

Aymestrey was part of the estate of Queen Edith, wife of Edward the Confessor, which was given to Ralph Mortimer (d.1115–27) before 1086. His son, Hugh (d.1181–85) gave the benefice to Odo, son of their steward, Oliver de Merlimond. Parts of the church were built in the twelfth century. It was possibly used as a stables, store and resting place prior to the battle and some of the dead were buried at Aymestrey. Inside the church is the Lingen tomb which commemorates Sir John Lingen and Elizabeth Burgh his wife. The Lingen family had been tenants of the Mortimers and Sir John fought for Edward at Mortimers Cross and helped him to assume the Crown.

The site of the Battle of Mortimers Cross, with Hereford Lane on the right

INNER MORTIMER TOUR

ABOVE: The nameplate on the gate of Blue Mantle Cottage

RIGHT: The tomb slab in Aymestrey church of Sir John Lingen, who fought at Mortimers Cross, and of his wife

What to see

The actual site of the battle has not yet been identified, though a recent archaeological project may yet reveal its whereabouts. It is assumed to be just south of the Mortimers Cross junction, in the vicinity of the stump of the Battle Oak and Blue Mantle Cottage (see p. 74). At the crossroads is the Mortimers Cross Inn where a visitor centre with walk information will be developed in due course.

In the apex of the road junction on the north side of Kingsland, where the road to the village forks off the A4110 opposite the rugby club, there is a monument erected in 1799 which records the details of the battle.

The parish church of St John the Baptist and St Alkmund in Aymestrey contains the tomb of Sir John Lingen, who fought at the Battle of Mortimers Cross, and his wife.

7) Kingsland

Location

Kingsland lies to the south of Mortimers Cross, down the A4110, and is found on a lane that branches off on the east side.

Mortimer connections

Domesday records that Ralph Mortimer (d.1115–27) owned some land within the manor of Kingsland. As its name suggests, Domesday indicates that the manor was 'land of the king'. Originally, in 660, Merewalh, king of the Magonsaete, a sub-kingdom of Mercia, had reserved Kingsland for his own use. It was owned later by Edward the Confessor, then William I. By the early 1100s it had been given to the de Braose family, who first built a motte and bailey castle on the site. Page 10 describes how de Braose first allied with Hugh Mortimer (d.1181–85) during the civil war of 1138–54 but then switched sides, leaving Wigmore isolated and vulnerable. King John is reported to have slept in Kingsland Castle, which was rebuilt after the Anarchy.

As related earlier (see p. 26) the castle and manor came into Mortimer possession through Roger Mortimer's marriage to Maud de Braose in 1247. Roger died at Kingsland in 1282, and Maud and her successors oversaw the building of the church.

What to see

The site of the motte and bailey castle is accessed through the churchyard. The site of the castle, which had an octagonal stone keep, can be seen from a footpath alongside the fence to its north. (The field in which the motte stands is glebe land to which the Church allows public access at the time of going to print. If this is still the case you can enter the field to walk around the motte.) You can also make out the outlines of the fishponds, which would have been used at the time of the Mortimers, on the river side of the bailey.

The church of St Michael and All Angels is today very much the same as when Maud and successors oversaw its building. It is a fine church to visit and of particular note in relation to the Mortimers are: the coat of arms associated with Maud in the fourteenth-century east window; the original splendid nave roof; the font, tomb recess and preaching cross which also date from the fourteenth century; the clergy board within the church that lists two younger sons of the Mortimer family as rectors in the early 1300s. As you enter the church the remarkable Volka Chapel on the left is likely to be the chantry chapel for one of those rectors, Walter Mortimer. Following the Battle of Mortimers Cross (see pp. 73–75), Edward IV founded two chantry chapels in Kingsland church, one for 'Our Lady' and the other for 'St Katherine', to 'pray for the souls of those slain in the battle of Mortimers Cross'. Prayers are still said every year in the Volka Chapel on 2 February.

Kingsland Castle motte (photograph © Logaston Press)

LEFT: Coat of arms of Maud de Braose depicted in stained glass at St Michael's Church, Kingsland
RIGHT: The Volka Chapel at Kingsland church (photograph © Logaston Press)

8) Shobdon

Location
The village is located on the B4362 towards Presteigne, a few miles after Mortimers Cross. Before you reach the village of Shobdon, follow signs to the Shobdon Arches. This route takes you along minor roads to a crossroads where you keep ahead on a lane across the Shobdon Court estate. Shobdon church is on the left with car parking beside the lane in front of the church. The Shobdon Arches are at the end of the tree-lined walk on the right as you reach the church.

Mortimer connections
Shobdon was another manor previously owned by Queen Edith and given to Ralph Mortimer (d.1115–27) before 1086. The building of the church in the 1130s at the time of the Anarchy by the Mortimers' steward, Oliver de Merlimond, the founding of the Priory that later became Wigmore Abbey, and Oliver's subsequent falling out with Hugh are described in detail on pp. 9–16.

What to see
Unfortunately, from our point of view, the church built by Oliver at Shobdon no longer exists as in 1752 the owner pulled it down, with the exception of the tower built in the thirteenth or fourteenth century under Mortimer patronage, and replaced it with a remarkable church in Rococo style. The twelfth-century font by the Herefordshire School of Romanesque Sculptors (see pp. 12–14) is still to be found inside the church.

Some of the most highly decorated elements of the original church by the Herefordshire School (the chancel arch, and north and south doorways) were re-erected as a folly about 400 metres north of the church, at the end of a tree-lined avenue – the Shobdon Arches, much weather-worn but still remarkable.

The site of the motte and bailey castle built by Hugh (d.1181–85) is a short way to the west of the church. Go along the main estate lane with a factory on the right. The motte is on the left and there is a stile onto the footpath by the farm gate.

The remains of the motte at Shobdon

The Shobdon Arches, comprising the rebuilt chancel arch (centre)
and north and south doorways to the Romanesque church

The lion of St Mark on the Romanesque font
inside the Strawberry Hill Gothic church

9) Pembridge

Location

The village of Pembridge is located along the A44. It is part of the north Herefordshire 'Black and White Trail' and has a number of fine buildings that have been dated to the period 1425–1525.

Mortimer connections

In 1230 the overlordship of Pembridge passed to the Mortimers as custodians of the de Braose estates following the execution of William de Braose by Llywelyn. It formally became part of the Mortimer estates when the de Pembridge family forfeited it for their support of Simon de Montfort against King Henry III in 1265, and it was granted instead to Roger Mortimer (d.1282). Whilst all the rest of their lands were restored to the de Pembridge family, Roger had forced them to sign Pembridge over to him permanently (done 'willingly' in court by Henry de Pembridge, whilst Roger held his sons captive!) indicating the value that he placed on it. Roger's widow, Maud, reputedly lived at Pembridge after his death and it was frequently used thereafter as a dower property for Mortimer widows – for example Margaret de Fiennes who survived her husband, Edmund, for 29 years from 1304 to 1333; followed immediately by Joan de Geneville, widow of Roger from 1330 to 1356.

Roger Mortimer (d.1330) was married at Pembridge on 20 September 1301, to Joan de Geneville, who brought large estates, including Ludlow Castle, to the Mortimers. It is said a comet appeared the following day, and could be seen for the next seven nights. The intriguing question is, why did they marry at Pembridge? (not Wigmore, Roger's home; or Ludlow, Joan's home). One possibility is that Roger and Joan were going to live at Pembridge after their wedding. Roger's parents were living at Wigmore and Joan did not formally inherit Ludlow until 1308, so the couple possibly needed their own place to live. Roger's grandmother, Maud, who reputedly lived at the moated site in Pembridge after the death of her husband, had died earlier in 1301, so the property was available for the couple. As with other places on the tour, the theory is plausible and a good 'story' but as yet there is no evidence one way or the other, so needs treating with caution. It is recorded that Roger, after his victorious return to England, was at Pembridge at the end of 1326: did he meet his wife, Joan, here? The Mortimers, possibly Roger and Joan, or possibly Roger's mother Margaret who held Pembridge as a dower property, supported the rebuilding of the church.

What to see

All that remains of the church in which Roger and Joan married are two built-up twelfth-century arches in the chancel, and the south window in the chancel by the altar, which dates from *c.*1240. Instead, you can see the church they built as they and their family paid for the current church of St Mary, constructed in the late 1320s/early 1330s. A seventeenth-century account relates that the original stained glass windows, which no longer exist, held the arms of Roger Mortimer, de Geneville and their son-in-law Sir Peter de Grandison, who married their daughter, Blanche, in June 1330, also in Pembridge.

There are a number of carved stone heads on both the inside and outside of the church. Some bear a strong resemblance to the ones in St George's, Orleton which were being carved at roughly the same time – particularly the one on the spring of the end arch by the door at Pembridge and the male royal at Orleton. These are both thought to portray a young Edward III. The carved head high up above the chancel arch has generated different theories on who it might represent – possibly Christ, possibly Edward II, or possibly Roger Mortimer (it's in the same place above the chancel arch as the Orleton head which might be of Roger – see discussion in the box on pp. 44–45).

In the chancel there are fourteenth-century stone effigies of members of the Gour family, who were active in the service of the Mortimers. They have been identified as Nicholas Gour, his son John and their wives. The effigies are important as they are elaborately costumed and provide an insight into the life and dress of people other than knights and clergy. John Gour was a local landowner who worked for the Mortimers from the 1350s until his death in the late 1370s, for most of that time serving as Steward. He is recorded as a witness to Mortimer charters, was an executor of Roger Mortimer's will in 1360 and was appointed the keeper of the Mortimer estates in the Marches for the period of the minority of Edmund (d.1381).

The church has a permanent display of the Pembridge Tapestries, embroidered by a local group to depict the history of Pembridge. The first four depict: Norman Pembridge, the Bell Tower, the Mortimers building St Mary's Church, and timber-framed houses following the destruction of Owain Glyn Dŵr.

Outside the church is the third detached bell tower on this tour. Larger than Yarpole's, the four huge timber corner posts were erected between 1207 and 1214. It is considered to be one of the finest detached bell towers and is structurally similar to ones found in Norway and Sweden. Like the one at Yarpole, the wooden structure was later encased in stone, this one in the fifteenth century.

Pembridge church (photographs © Robert Anderson)

ABOVE LEFT: A head on the second column to the left of the entrance door (the north side of the aisle), that might represent Philippa of Hainault, wife of Edward III

ABOVE: A head on the first column to the left of the entrance door (the north side of the aisle), that may represent Edward III

LEFT: The head above the chancel arch, that might represent Edward II, Roger Mortimer (d.1330) or Jesus

BELOW: Looking east up the nave to the chancel

Pembridge church: On the left of the photograph is the detached belfry (one of three on the tour). It has huge timber corner posts erected 1207–14, and the structure was encased in stone in the fifteenth century (photograph © Robert Anderson)

Pembridge church: the lady chapel in the south transept (note the surviving painted decoration on the wall to the right of the east window, of white roses on a red ground) (photograph © Robert Anderson)

The remains of the motte and bailey castle, which consists of a large mound surrounded by a wide, deep moat, can be seen from the churchyard behind the church. The site, which lies in the private grounds of Court House Farm, was excavated in 2004. Research suggests that the mound probably dates from the late eleventh/early twelfth century and was the chief seat of the de Pembridge family before being taken over by Roger Mortimer (d.1282) in 1265. During this period the function of the moated site changed from being a castle in the twelfth century to a fortified manor house by about 1300, and appears to have become a favoured residence of the Mortimers. The archaeological excavations revealed the courses of stone walls, probably the foundations of a substantial stone building and evidence of destruction and reconstruction. Other findings included a piece of Roman tile, early medieval pottery and plasterwork, a knife blade and an iron stirrup.

10) Presteigne and Stapleton

Location
Presteigne is on the B4362 from Mortimers Cross, just over the border in Wales, and is the only Welsh town that is east of Offa's Dyke. The Warden (the site of the motte and bailey castle) is signposted on the hill off the west side of the B4355 which bypasses the town centre. St Andrew's Church is found by turning north-east off the road through the town centre and is on the left just before the river crossing, having passed the Judge's Lodging on the right.

Stapleton Castle is about a mile further along the same road and back in Herefordshire. (NB although the ruins of Stapleton Castle are privately owned, they can be seen from nearby lanes and footpaths. The site is open a few days of the year through the National Garden Scheme or by arrangement through the Judge's Lodging and Tourist Information Centre.)

Mortimer connections
After the Conquest in 1066, Presteigne belonged to the lords of Richards Castle, who first built a castle at the site now called The Warden. The castle and manor were seized from them in 1144 during the Anarchy and subsequently passed into the control of the de Braose family. When William de Braose was executed in 1230 without a male heir and leaving four young daughters, the castle and the church of St Andrew came into the control of Ralph Mortimer

The site of Presteigne Castle on The Warden (photograph © Logaston Press)

of Wigmore (d.1246) as custodian of the de Braose lands (Ralph had also married Gwladus Ddu, who was the widow of Reginald de Braose, William's father). Mortimer control of Presteigne was cemented in 1247 when Ralph's son, Roger (d.1282), married Maud de Braose, who had inherited Presteigne from her father, William. From the thirteenth century the patronage of the church was vested in the canons of Wigmore Abbey.

The castle, which had probably never been built in stone, was sacked in 1262 by the forces of Llywelyn ap Gruffudd, and not rebuilt. As an Anglo-Norman lordship on the border with Wales, Presteigne was vulnerable to attacks from the Welsh and was sacked again, this time by the forces of Owain Glyn Dŵr, in 1402.

When the castle at Presteigne had passed out of the control of the lords of Richards Castle in 1144, in order to maintain their influence in the area they built another castle nearby at Stapleton, which subsequently passed into the ownership of the Mortimers of Richards Castle.

What to see
The site of the motte and bailey castle at Presteigne can be seen within the late eighteenth- and nineteenth-century landscaped gardens called The Warden, at the top of the hill with fine views over the town and surrounding countryside.

LEFT: The Mortimer tomb lid in Presteigne church. RIGHT: The east window of Presteigne church showing the location of the possible Mortimer-related plaque, with, above left, the plaque itself

The ruins of the medieval Stapleton Castle were incorporated into a seventeenth-century house (© Paul R. Davis)

St Andrew's Church, which dates from pre-Conquest times and contains some Saxon remains, was under the control of the Mortimers from the 1230s and has a rare collection of possible Mortimer artefacts: inside, in the north aisle, there is a Mortimer foliate tomb lid; on the external south wall there is a Mortimer of Wigmore coat of arms; and on the external wall above the east window a stone plaque reads 'M.P.L. 1244'. It has been suggested that MPL is an abbreviation for *Mortimer Posuit Libeus* Dŵr 'this part of the church Mortimer had the pleasure to erect in 1244'. However, the age of this plaque is not certain, there is no evidence of substantial building work in the 1240s, and the numerals '1244' seem to have been added much later to an earlier inscription, as they appear newer and are of a style not in use until 200 years later – so the plaque is a bit of a mystery. The present nave was built *c*.1320, when a south aisle was also added which connected the main body of the church to the tower, and a new larger chancel constructed. The colours of the 1st Radnorshire Rifle Volunteers are displayed in the church; at their centre is a representation of the arms of Radnorshire which were based on the coat of arms of the Mortimers.

The Mortimer coat of arms on the outside of Presteigne church

The castle at Stapleton, set on a prominent hill, fell into decay but the remains of the castle were incorporated into a seventeenth-century house. In turn this too fell into decay. As noted above, the ruins of the house on the top of a hill are privately owned but can be seen from neighbouring lanes and footpaths and visited on certain days or by arrangement.

11 New and Old Radnor

Location
New Radnor is located on the north side of the A44, eight miles to the south-west of Presteigne; Old Radnor is on the south side of the A44, three miles to the east of New Radnor.

Mortimer Connections

In 1066, Radnor was an Anglo-Saxon borough seized by the Normans as a result of their conquest of England. In the 1090s, the lordship of Radnor was granted by William (Rufus) II to the de Braose family. By the early thirteenth century, the de Braose were one of the most powerful Marcher families; however, their influence was weakened when they fell out with King John. In 1230, William de Braose was hanged by Llywelyn ab Iorwerth, the prince of Gwynedd, after he was found in the chambers of Llywelyn's wife. Although William was survived by four daughters, he had no sons, so the inheritance was divided between the daughters. As three of them were still children, the lands and castles were given to the custody of others. By 1235, the castle and lordship of Radnor had been granted to Ralph Mortimer (d.1246), who had married Gwladus Ddu, the daughter of Llywelyn ab Iorwerth and widow of William's father, to hold in custody for the heiress, Maud de Braose.

In 1247, Ralph Mortimer's son, Roger (d.1282), married Maud de Braose, and thus the castle and lordship passed into the ownership of the Mortimer family. This was the first in a series of marriages that, over the next century, would bring the Mortimers extensive lands and titles across the Marches, England and Ireland, creating a vast empire of estates. In addition to Radnor, Maud's inheritance included Narberth in the south-west Marches and a third share in each of Haverford and St Clears. In 1256, Roger was granted 'murage' for five years to build walls round the borough of Radnor, establishing the new town.

In England, increasing tensions between Henry III and the barons led to the civil conflict of the Barons' Wars, during which Simon de Montfort sent his sons to ally with Llywelyn ap Gruffudd. Together they captured the castle and town of Radnor in 1264, burning both to the ground – the fourth time this had happened. Roger soon regained Radnor and, at the height of his influence following the Battle of Evesham, he withdrew Radnor from the administrative and judicial structures of Herefordshire, thus turning it into a Marcher lordship in which he exercised regal-like powers. It remained in Mortimer possession until the death in 1425 of Edmund Mortimer, 5th earl of March, when it passed to Richard, duke of York. When his son was crowned Edward IV, the lordship of Radnor became the property of the Crown.

Photogrammetric image of Radnor Castle at New Radnor, showing the extent to which the castle dominated the town (© CPAT image 4236-3415, photograph by Julian Ravest)

What to see

Whilst there are no masonry remains, the vast mound of New Radnor Castle still dominates the town and surrounding plain. The castle saw plenty of action during the conflicts with the Welsh, changing hands 12 times in only 80 years, on four occasions being substantially destroyed. The size, scale and commanding position of the site are well worth exploring. In the town, to the south and west, it is possible to see glimpses of the town walls built by Roger Mortimer. Although St Mary's Church is Victorian, it contains two medieval effigies – it has been argued that the male one is of Einion o'r Porth, a Welsh prince who held Radnor for a period, whilst the female effigy could be Maud de Braose. In St Stephen's Church, Old Radnor, the stone slab set into the nave floor and decorated with a floriated cross, has been identified by some as the tombstone of Hugh Mortimer, rector of Old Radnor 1257–90. Despite the names, it has been argued that 'New Radnor' is the older settlement on the basis that it was the dominant castle and the 'New' refers to the new town established by Roger Mortimer.

The much-worn effigy, possibly of Maud de Braose, in New Radnor church

LEFT: St Stephen's Church, Old Radnor.
RIGHT: The slab set into the nave floor, which may be the tombstone of Hugh Mortimer

12 Cefnllys Castles

Location
About two miles east of Llandrindod Wells. SO 089 614.

Mortimer Connections
The Welsh district of Maelienydd, which bordered Wigmore to the west, was the obvious target for Mortimer expansion and acquisition of more lands. First seized in the 1090s, they built the castle at Cymaron; however, the Mortimer position in Maelienydd was never secure, with control passing back and forth for nearly two centuries; indeed, during those 180 years, the Mortimers had control for only 80 years. During one such period, after the death in 1240 of Llywelyn ab Iorwerth, the prince of Gwynedd who had extended his control over much of Wales, the 11-year-old Roger Mortimer (d.1282) was given responsibility in 1242 to build a castle on the northern end of the natural ridge at Cefnllys, possibly extending a castle first built by Llywelyn. In 1262, the castle was seized and destroyed by men loyal to Llywelyn ap Gruffudd. Although the 1267 Treaty of Montgomery gave Roger permission to rebuild the castle, he built a new one at the southern end, eliciting vociferous complaints from Llywelyn ap Gruffudd. Cefnllys remained in the possession of the Mortimers until it passed to the Yorkists, and then to the Crown.

The natural ridge at Cefnllys. The site of the original castle of 1242 is at the north (near) end; at the south end Roger Mortimer, after 1267, built the second castle which caused complaints from Llywelyn ap Gruffudd (© CPAT image 4236-2025, photograph by Julian Ravest)

What to see

The site of two castles in one setting, at each end of the natural steep-sided ridge, with magnificent views across the valleys and Radnorshire hills.

13 Abbey Cwm Hir

Location

Six miles north of Llandrindod Wells, along a minor road west off the A483.

Mortimer connections

The Cistercian Abbey was founded in 1176 by Cadwallon ap Madog during a lengthy period of native rule of Maelienydd that lasted over 40 years. After Roger Mortimer (d.1214) reconquered the district in 1195, he became the benefactor of the Abbey, issuing a charter in 1200 to confirm the existing grants of land to the abbey and to make new ones. The charter has a standard clause that the grant is to support the monks to pray for the salvation of the souls of Mortimer and his family; an unusual clause, however, states that it is also so that they may pray for the souls of 'those of his men who lost their

The picturesque ruins of Abbey Cwm Hir

lives in this very conquest.' The abbey nave measures 74m in length, one of the largest in Britain, though the transepts were never completed. Dr David Stephenson has argued convincingly that it was built under the patronage of Roger Mortimer in the early years of the thirteenth century. Although Maelienydd was regained by the Welsh for long periods in the thirteenth century, the district and the abbey remained in Mortimer hands until 1425.

What to see
Abbey Cwm Hir is located in a beautiful setting by the river in a picturesque valley surrounded by wooded hills. Some walls still remain, and a plaque commemorates the reputed burial site of Llywelyn ap Gruffudd. After the Reformation, some of the piers and arches were removed to be re-erected in the church at Llanidloes, where they can still be seen.

14 TINBOETH CASTLE

Location
Above the A483, roughly 11 miles north of Llandrindod Wells. SO 090 755.

Mortimer connections
Tinboeth Castle was built between 1267 and possibly 1277 (certainly by 1282), when Maelienydd was in Mortimer control, and would remain so permanently. The castle is also known as Dinbaud (Maud's Castle) suggesting that Maud

Aerial view of Tinboeth Castle, looking south-east
(© CPAT image 962-001, photograph by Julian Ravest)

de Braose, the wife of Roger Mortimer (d.1282), may have been involved in its establishment. Although it was still in use in 1316 and 1322, it quickly ceased to be a functioning castle. The end of native rule in Wales, which brought a cessation to the conflicts and volatility in Maelienydd, shortly after the castle was built, quickly ended the military purposes of this isolated fortress. As no hamlet appears to have formed around the site, and lacking a military or political raison d'être, abandonment and decay rapidly followed.

What to see
Part of the gatehouse is still standing, the last forlorn fragment of the now largely collapsed twin-towered gatehouse; other fragments of walls can be seen perched on a hilltop with commanding views of the surrounding area.

15 Cymaron Castle

Location
On an unclassified road, approximately one-and-a-half miles west south-west of Llanbister Road Station SO 152 704.

Mortimer Connections

The Mortimers probably built a castle at Cymaron in the 1090s when they first seized the cantref of Maelienydd, with Cymaron becoming their main castle in the lordship for over a century. This can be deduced from the Welsh chronicles, the Brut y Tywysogyon, which record that in 1144 Hugh Mortimer (d.1181–85) repaired the castle of Cymaron, and for a second time gained possession of Maelienydd. As the Mortimers had been absent from the country for most of the preceding 44 years (during which time Maelienydd was regained by the native Welsh rulers), it is safe to say that it was first built in the 1090s during the first conquest of Maelienydd. By 1155, though, it had been retaken by the Welsh and remained in their hands for 40 years. During this period, the men of Hugh's son, Roger Mortimer (d.1214), murdered the ruler of Maelienydd, Cadwallon ap Madog, in 1179. Roger was imprisoned by the king and his men executed for the crime. The king also seized Cymaron castle because of the debts owed by Cadwallon to the Crown; however, his sons seized it back three years later.

In 1195, Roger Mortimer retook Cymaron when he seized back all of Maelienydd, with the king giving him £20 to refortify the castle. After the death of Roger in 1214, the following year Llywelyn ab Iorwerth retook Maelienydd and destroyed Cymaron Castle. The castle appears never to have been rebuilt and was subsequently replaced by the castle at Cefnllys when that

An aerial view of Cymaron Castle showing the farm standing in the former castle bailey, with the motte to the right (© CPAT image 1112-002, photograph by Julian Ravest)

was built by the Mortimers in 1242, following their seizure of Maelienydd the previous year, after the death of Llywelyn in 1240. The manor, however, continued and the Mortimers built a courthouse at Cymaron by the end of the thirteenth century.

What to see
The site of the castle is privately owned, with a farmhouse occupying the bailey; however, the earthworks and mound can be seen from the adjacent lane and footpaths.

16) Pilleth and the Battle of Bryn Glas

Location
Pilleth is five miles from Presteigne along the B4356. On the south-west side of the road just before the small settlement a public footpath takes you to Castell Foel Allt, the site of a motte and bailey castle located on the river Lugg, which was an early Mortimer outlier castle. St Mary's Church and Bryn Glas are up a track a little further along on the opposite side.

Mortimer connections
Pilleth, in Wales, was a western outlier of the Wigmore lordship. It is thought that the castle of Foel Allt was built by Ralph Mortimer (d.1115–27) sometime after 1086. There is, though, only one known reference to it when it was a residence of the dowager Lady Mortimer in 1341.

As described earlier (see pp. 63–64), the Battle of Pilleth (or Bryn Glas) was fought on 22 June 1402 between the armies of Owain Glyn Dŵr, seeking to establish Welsh independence, and Sir Edmund Mortimer (uncle of the child Edmund Mortimer, 5th earl of March, who was in the custody of the king) who led the local militia, largely made up from tenants of the Mortimer estates and possibly totalling some 2,000. The slaughter was said to have been horrendous, and accounts put the numbers killed at between 200 and 1,100. Reports also quickly circulated that the Welsh women accompanying Owain's army had 'obscenely mutilated' many of the bodies of the fallen. The battle, and its outcome, was a decisive event not only in that the defeat of an English force gave credibility to Owain's rebellion but also it marked the decline of Mortimer military power.

What to see

A footpath, which heads north from the road at Pilleth, on the Whitton side of the settlement, passes close by the motte of Castell Foel Allt.

The overall location of the Battle of Pilleth on the hill of Bryn Glas and St Mary's Church is best viewed from the site of the castle, looking in a northerly direction, as you can appreciate the whole terrain and the steepness of the hill faced by Sir Edmund's forces.

Castell Foel Allt (photograph © Logaston Press)

The whitewashed church of St Mary, Pilleth

Local tradition indicates that the bodies were buried in mass graves on the hillside, and six Wellingtonia trees (four survive) were planted in the nineteenth century to indicate one of the sites. Although no records exist to substantiate this claim, it is quite possibly true, as many human bones have been turned up on the hillside. The trees can still be seen on the hillside behind Pilleth church.

The church of St Mary our Lady of Pilleth suffered badly in the battle and was gutted by fire in the nineteenth century. It was a place of medieval pilgrimage for the healing properties of the well outside the church.

17) Knighton

Location
Knighton is located on the junction of the A4113 and A488, just on the Welsh side of the border between England and Wales. It is often referred to as 'the town-on-the-dyke' as it is the only settlement actually on Offa's Dyke.

Mortimer connections
Knighton was an early Norman Conquest and settlement after 1066, and was founded by Hugh the Ass, a follower of William the Conqueror. After this it was inherited by the Chandos family. Knighton was forfeited to the Crown following an unsuccessful rebellion by Roger Chandos in 1186. For a time it was held by the de Braose family; however, in 1207 King John took it from them and gave Knighton to Roger Mortimer (d.1214). A few months later, Roger was ordered to pass Knighton to the Sheriff of Shropshire, who retained control until 1215 when Llywelyn ab Iorwerth ('the Great'), in alliance with de Braose, took and destroyed both castles. Although the sheriff was no longer in occupation, Roger's son, Hugh (d.1227), gave him land in exchange for Knighton Castle. Hugh then tried to secure control through the courts, without success.

Mortimer ownership of Knighton was not finally confirmed until 1230, with the marriage between Gwladus Ddu, the daughter of Llywelyn, and Hugh's brother and heir, Ralph Mortimer (d.1246). A few weeks later, King Henry III granted Ralph the right by charter to hold a fair in Knighton. Ralph was then probably responsible for rebuilding the castle, and Knighton remained in Mortimer control except for short periods when captured by the Welsh.

The motte of Bryn y Castell

Towns along the border, such as Knighton, Knucklas and Presteigne, were centres of Anglo-Norman population and culture in the midst of Celtic areas, aiding the process of colonisation. It is not surprising that they became a focus of Welsh hatred and were often the targets for destruction. Knighton was sacked by Llywelyn ap Gruffudd in 1260 and two years later in 1262 he captured the castle. By 1273 the castle was uninhabitable as rooms had to be booked in the town for a meeting of the Mortimer council. Although Roger (d.1282) was granted 'murage' to build walls around the town in 1260 and 1277 there is no evidence this was done. Knighton was sacked again during the uprisings of Owain Glyn Dŵr at the start of the fifteenth century.

Despite this, Knighton was part of the dower estates of both Maud de Braose (between 1282 and 1301) and Margaret de Fiennes (between 1304 and 1334).

What to see
There are two castles in Knighton. The origins of both are unclear and there are two theories as to which was the first to be built. One theory is that Bryn y Castell, located on the western outskirts of the present town, was the original castle built by the Chandos lords to control a strategic route along the Teme Valley out of England into Wales; then *c.*1190 a new castle was erected 500 metres to the west, in the current town centre, by William de Braose, and rebuilt by the Mortimers. The alternative theory is that the original castle was on the town centre site and Bryn y Castell was constructed after 1215 to counter the threat to Wigmore and the Marches from Llywelyn who had seized Knighton.

Whichever theory is correct, Bryn y Castell was built to dominate the area and control the strategic route along the Teme Valley, and was certainly redundant after the Mortimers started to rebuild the town centre castle after 1230. The motte of Bryn y Castell, which is accessed from the footpath behind the community centre opposite the cattle market, can be viewed and walked on. There is little to see of Knighton Castle, located at the top of The Narrows, as it is now ringed by private houses and the fire station, with no access between them. There are glimpses of the motte between the buildings.

18) Knucklas

Location
Knucklas is two miles north-west of Knighton along the B4355.

Mortimer connections
Although Llywelyn gave Knighton to Ralph Mortimer (d.1246), he retained control of much of Maelienydd, including Knucklas. The Mortimers didn't take control of Knucklas until after Llywelyn's death in 1240. Analysis by Paul Remfry suggests that Llywelyn possibly first built the castle at Knucklas sometime between 1218 and 1234, and subsequently Ralph is recorded in the Wigmore Chronicle as substantially rebuilding it in the early 1240s. Its existence was short-lived as it was destroyed by Llywelyn ap Gruffudd in 1262 and never rebuilt – it is not listed in the castles confiscated in 1322, and in 1406 was regarded as a lordship without a castle. The borough of Knucklas was also one of the smallest in Wales and had a very short existence. It was most likely founded in the 1240s as an adjunct to the castle, and may well have ceased existence in 1262 after the castle was captured and destroyed.

Looking along Knucklas railway viaduct

What to see

The castle, built probably on the site of an iron-age fort, consisted of a small, square masonry tower with circular, angular turrets and a barbican wall. Now, though, only the castle mound on top of Castle Hill remains, full of lumps and bumps, which is accessed up fairly steep paths from the village.

Knucklas Castle site looking north across the Teme valley, with a modern sculpture, the Dragon's Tooth.

Looking up the Teme valley into Wales from the site of Knucklas Castle

To find the castle site, coming from Knighton on the B4355 Newtown road, take the first turning left, signposted for Knucklas. At the Castle Inn bear right and when the lane bends right over a bridge over a stream you will see a no-through road sign and phone box in front of you. Follow this lane up, running parallel to the railway line, till you see a small layby in an old quarry on the right where you may be able to park. The entrance to the castle is a few yards further on along a footpath on your right. It is worth the walk, though, to see the commanding views from the top over the Teme and Heyope Valleys towards the hills of Radnorshire and Shropshire, and Offa's Dyke. There are also views over the Knucklas railway viaduct with its magnificent turrets, some of the stone for which came from the castle ruins. It makes you think that if the Mortimers had had a railway set, this is what it would have looked like.

An enterprising and imaginative community cooperative is managing the site whilst also raising funds to purchase it for the community.

19) Lingen

Location
Lingen, about three miles west of Wigmore, is located on unclassified roads, roughly in the centre of a triangle formed by Wigmore, Presteigne and Knighton. The site of Limebrook Priory is roughly one mile to the south, a short way along the lane to Upper Lye and Aymestrey.

Mortimer connections
At the time of Domesday in 1086, Lingen was held by Turstin as a tenant of Ralph Mortimer (d.1115–27). By the 1100s it had come under the control of the Lingen family, knights in the service of the Mortimers, who owned it until 1583. Sir Ralph Lingen was a knight in the service of Edmund Mortimer (d.1381) in the 1370s. In 1461 John Lingen was one of Edward's key leaders at the Battle of Mortimers Cross, afterwards supporting his claim to the throne as Edward IV, and was later knighted. Sir John Lingen's tomb is in Aymestrey church.

Limebrook Priory was founded *c.*1189 as an Augustinian nunnery, and two Mortimer sisters were canonesses there – Joan and Elizabeth, who were daughters of Edmund Mortimer (d.1304) and sisters of Roger Mortimer (d.1330), who gave financial support (the revenues of the church of Stoke Bliss) to the priory.

What to see

Immediately north of the church, accessed by a footpath from the churchyard, is a good example of a motte and bailey castle, probably built by Turstin. The motte has traces that may represent a shell keep and gatehouse.

The current church was constructed in the nineteenth century, but retains the font and a piscina (a stone basin used for rinsing the chalice, located on the right-hand side of the sanctuary) from the original thirteenth-century church.

The site of Limebrook Priory

The site of Limebrook Priory can be seen alongside a lane in a quiet location, but lies on private ground. All that remains of the priory buildings is a portion of wall, adjacent to the lane, that was part of a long rectangular room, together with evidence of walls and buildings in the adjoining field. A section of the walling of the barn alongside the road may also have been part of one of the priory's buildings.

An aerial view of the motte and bailey of Lingen Castle (© Paul R. Davis)

20) Leintwardine

Location
Leintwardine is located on the A4113, near the junction with the A4110.

Mortimer connections
The origins of Leintwardine go back to an early settlement on an important crossing of the river Teme, which later became occupied and fortified by the Romans. Before the Conquest of 1066 it was a royal manor held by King Edward the Confessor, but by 1086 Leintwardine was held by Ralph Mortimer (d.1115–27).

St Mary Magdalene Church in the centre of the village, was begun in the late twelfth century, possibly on the site of a Saxon minster, and was given by Hugh Mortimer (d.1181–85) to the canons of Wigmore Abbey. It is said that from 1184 the abbot led a yearly procession from the abbey to the church on the Feast of the Nativity.

Roger Mortimer (d.1330) funded building works and at the height of his power in December 1328 granted lands and rent to the value of 100 marks (£66) for nine chantry priests to sing masses daily at St Mary Magdalene for the souls of King Edward III and Queen Philippa, Queen Isabella (Edward III's mother), Bishop Burghersh, himself, his wife Joan, his children and their ancestors. Two months later he increased the resources to pay for a tenth priest.

King Edward III made two pilgrimages to Leintwardine in 1353, making an offering of 20s on one visit and laying a cloth of gold before the statue of the Virgin Mary on the other. For such a rural country settlement, the amount of Mortimer and royal attention is extraordinary.

What to see
The church was added to over the years with help from the Mortimers. The tower was built in the fourteenth century. Although Roger Mortimer (d.1330) made the endowments for the chantry priests in 1328/9, Dr Ian Mortimer has concluded that the chantry chapel called the Mortimer Chapel was not in fact built until 1352–3 and the visits by Edward III marked its completion.

Some have speculated that the choir stalls and the misericords (the carvings under the choir stall seats) may well have come from Wigmore Abbey at the Dissolution, but it seems more likely that they were specially produced for the Mortimer Chapel. There are five misericords on the south side, depicting the Resurrection, the Annunciation, angels and wrestlers.

CLOCKWISE FROM TOP: Leintwardine church: to the left is the large chantry chapel on the north side of the chancel; part of the c.1500 stone reredos; the choir stalls, which might have come from Wigmore Abbey; the richly-carved c.1500 nave roof (photographs © Robert Anderson)

21) Pipe Aston

Location
Pipe Aston is located midway along the seven-mile-long unclassified road between Wigmore and Ludlow, now the quiet, scenic, back route between the two former centres of Mortimer power. Leinthall Earls and Starkes are closer to Wigmore.

Mortimer connections
Pipe Aston (it was just Aston in the Mortimer period – the 'Pipe' refers to its period at the centre of the manufacture of clay pipes for about 200 years from c.1630) belonged to Ralph Mortimer (d.1115–27) in 1086. Close to the boundary between the lands of Wigmore and Ludlow and on the direct route between the two strongholds, Pipe Aston is the location of two castle sites. The feuds between Hugh Mortimer (d.1181–85) and Joce de Dinan of Ludlow during the Anarchy of the twelfth century, are described on pp. 11, 12 and 15. The church of St Giles was built in the twelfth century under Mortimer patronage.

Leinthall Earls and Leinthall Starkes both belonged to Ralph Mortimer at the time of Domesday and have churches that originated in the twelfth century.

What to see
The small twelfth-century church of St Giles, Pipe Aston is particularly notable for the arched stone carving (a tympanum) above the entrance door, which is by the Herefordshire School of Sculptors (see pp. 12–14), as is the font inside. The nave has an original Norman wall painting and red flower motifs which look as if they could be medieval wallpaper.

The site of the motte and bailey castle, known as the Pipe Aston Tump, is clearly seen from the lane c.100 metres north of the church. Its location suggests that its purpose was possibly to warn of attack from Ludlow and provide initial defence to the Wigmore estates and it is likely to have been of use during the period of the Anarchy in the mid twelfth century and the warring feuds between Hugh Mortimer (d.1181–85) and Joce de Dinan, who held Ludlow. The second site, c.200 metres further along the lane towards Ludlow on the right-hand side, is much harder to make out amongst the jumble of hedges, brambles and trees, and may have been a temporary siege castle set up to besiege the Mortimers' castle.

ABOVE: Aston church, with details of the tympanum (LEFT) and font (RIGHT). The carving on the font is upside down, suggesting the carved stone had another purpose, perhaps as a cross base.
BELOW: The motte that stands near to the church

22) Ludlow and Ludford Bridge

Location
Ludlow is located off the A49. The castle and St Laurence's Church are at the top of the hill at either end of the town centre/market place (access to St Laurence's is through a small alley between shops at the corner of the Buttercross). Ludford Bridge crosses the river Teme at the southern edge of the town, down through the Broad Gate. Over the river is the settlement of Ludford.

Mortimer connections
As another major stronghold only seven miles from Wigmore and the centre of a wealthy lordship, there were inevitably disputes between the Mortimers of Wigmore and the lords of Ludlow, particularly during the Anarchy in the early twelfth century (see pp. 9–15 for more information).

Ludlow Castle was first built in the late eleventh century by the de Lacy family. When the last male de Lacy died *c.*1240, the estates were divided between two daughters, with the castle and part of the town eventually coming into the possession of the de Genevilles. Following Roger Mortimer's (d.1330) marriage to Joan de Geneville in 1301, Ludlow Castle came into the ownership of the Mortimers in 1308. Roger spent some of his wealth on extensive building works to make the castle more palatial. He was responsible for constructing the new Great Chamber Block, the Garderobe Tower, and also St Peter's Chapel in memory of his escape from the Tower of London. Page 49 recounts Roger's visit in 1329 to Ludlow, and to his wife who was the lady of the castle, when he was accompanied by his lover, Queen Isabella, and the young King Edward III.

After Roger's downfall and execution, his wife, Joan, held Ludlow as her own inheritance until her death in 1356. By then Ludlow was becoming the Mortimers' preferred home in the Marches, but as leading earls in the country, in line of succession to the throne and with vast estates in three countries, the Mortimer earls spent much less time here than had earlier generations.

When Edmund Mortimer died childless in 1425, the vast Mortimer inheritance passed to his sister's young son, Richard, duke of York. Ludlow became one of Richard's favourite homes, the centre of his affairs in the Marches and where two of his sons grew up – one to become King of England. Pages 70–71 describe the circumstances that led to Richard asserting his claim to

Ludlow Castle seen from Whitcliffe Common across the Teme

the throne (based largely on his Mortimer descent), the outbreak of civil war (the Wars of the Roses), the collapse and flight of the Yorkists at the 'Rout of Ludford Bridge' (1459) and subsequent devastation and pillaging in Ludlow by the Royalist Lancastrian forces.

Following the death of Richard, his eldest son, Edward, who had been brought up at Ludlow, took over the leadership of the Yorkist cause and after winning the Battle of Mortimers Cross (1461) rode to London where he was proclaimed king. Ludlow and the rest of the Mortimer estates and titles passed into the royal family. Shortly after his coronation Edward IV spent a week at Ludlow, granted the town a new charter and personally contributed to further rebuilding of St Laurence's.

In his turn Edward IV sent his eldest son to be brought up at Ludlow between 1473 and 1483. Prince Edward set out from Ludlow on hearing of the death of his father, to travel to London to be crowned but was intercepted on the way by his uncle (who was afraid of the prince coming under the influence of his mother's extensive Woodville family), placed in the Tower with his brother, and eventually disappeared.

When Prince Edward, aged three, had gone to live in Ludlow Castle with his own court, his affairs were entrusted to a 'Prince's Council' which subsequently developed into the main agent of royal authority in Wales and the Marches. Henry VII's eldest son, Prince Arthur, the Prince of Wales was granted the castle, lordship and town of Ludlow, dying in the castle in 1502, shortly after his marriage to Catherine of Aragon, who later married Arthur's younger brother, Henry VIII. During 1525–28, Henry and Catherine's daughter, the Princess Mary, lived in the castle for three winters with her court. The Council in the Marches of Wales administered Wales and the border regions until 1689.

What to see
Ludlow Castle is privately owned and there is an admission fee. It is one of the best ruined castles in the country as the remains are substantial enough for you to be able to walk through rooms and to climb towers that give you a strong feel for life some 600 to 900 years ago.

There are open-access footpaths around the outside of the walls of the bailey, which take you through the remains of St Peter's Chapel built by Roger Mortimer (d.1330), and which, on the opposite side of the castle, give a good external view of the Garderobe Tower and Great Chamber Block that he built.

Inside the castle, you can go into Mortimer's Tower (though, as explained on p. 12 it is not where Hugh Mortimer [d.1181–85] was kept prisoner as it was not built until 100 years later, in the mid thirteenth century). The remarkable round chapel in the inner bailey was built in the 1150s, and is a building seemingly unique in Britain. You can walk through Roger's Great Chamber block and the remarkable Garderobe Tower, which was built outside and breaking through the Norman curtain wall to provide the extra accommodation needed by Roger, who entertained lavishly. The tower had a number of bedrooms, each with its own garderobe (toilet), an unusual luxury. Visitors can see inside the Great Hall where Roger, Joan and their successors held great feasts. Collectively this range of buildings is considered one of the finest examples of its period in the country. There is a tradition that when Edward IV's son lived at Ludlow between 1473–83 he resided in buildings now replaced by the Tudor Lodgings to the right of the Great Chamber Block. In 1502, Prince Arthur and his bride Catherine of Aragon lived in the top floor of the solar wing after their marriage.

The parish church of St Laurence, often described as the 'Cathedral of the Marches', is a large, magnificent church that reflects the patronage of the York family, particularly King Edward IV, and also the wealth of Ludlow in

Ludlow Castle from the external walkway, showing St Peter's Chapel and Mortimer's Tower

the fifteenth century when it was significantly rebuilt. The superb Victorian stained glass west window depicts various lords of Ludlow, including Joce de Dinan, Roger Mortimer (d.1330), Edmund Mortimer (d.1381) and their coats of arms, the Yorkist lords, kings and princes, and Arthur, Prince of Wales. In the older north aisle are three roundels which are the oldest stained glass in the church, dating from $c.1320$ – they depict the coats of arms of Theobald de Verdon, his first wife Matilda Mortimer (sister of Roger, d.1330) and second wife Elizabeth Clare. In the chancel a memorial tablet of 2002 commemorates the 500th anniversary of the funeral of Prince Arthur and the burial of his heart in St Laurence's. Much of St Laurence's was rebuilt around 1450, including the impressive misericords (the small wooden shelves, with intricate carvings, that provided an element of support for people who were standing during the extremely long services). The chancel ceiling also dates from this time when Richard, duke of York, owned the town and castle. His badge of the 'falcon and fetterlock' is to be found on one of the misericords in the chancel and is also prominent as a roof boss at the west end of the chancel. Other misericords display the badges of Richard II and Henry VI as well as the feathers of the Prince of Wales. On the chancel roof is a boss displaying the white lion of March. There are also tombs and effigies of presidents and officers of the Council of the Marches.

The tower of St Laurence's Church, Ludlow, stands proud above the buildings that jostle around it

Ludlow Castle from the external walkway, showing St Peter's Chapel and Mortimer's Tower

the fifteenth century when it was significantly rebuilt. The superb Victorian stained glass west window depicts various lords of Ludlow, including Joce de Dinan, Roger Mortimer (d.1330), Edmund Mortimer (d.1381) and their coats of arms, the Yorkist lords, kings and princes, and Arthur, Prince of Wales. In the older north aisle are three roundels which are the oldest stained glass in the church, dating from *c.*1320 – they depict the coats of arms of Theobald de Verdon, his first wife Matilda Mortimer (sister of Roger, d.1330) and second wife Elizabeth Clare. In the chancel a memorial tablet of 2002 commemorates the 500th anniversary of the funeral of Prince Arthur and the burial of his heart in St Laurence's. Much of St Laurence's was rebuilt around 1450, including the impressive misericords (the small wooden shelves, with intricate carvings, that provided an element of support for people who were standing during the extremely long services). The chancel ceiling also dates from this time when Richard, duke of York, owned the town and castle. His badge of the 'falcon and fetterlock' is to be found on one of the misericords in the chancel and is also prominent as a roof boss at the west end of the chancel. Other misericords display the badges of Richard II and Henry VI as well as the feathers of the Prince of Wales. On the chancel roof is a boss displaying the white lion of March. There are also tombs and effigies of presidents and officers of the Council of the Marches.

The tower of St Laurence's Church, Ludlow, stands proud above the buildings that jostle around it

St Laurence's Church, Ludlow

ABOVE: The Mortimer coat of arms depicted in stained glass

RIGHT: Prince Arthur, the elder brother of Henry VIII, as depicted in stained glass

BELOW: Misericord of the Falcon and Fetterlock, the personal badge of Richard, duke of York

The town of Ludlow was created in the eleventh and twelfth centuries by the de Lacy family and is a classic Norman castle town laid out in a clear grid pattern. Ludlow thrived as a town and during the Mortimer period in the 1370s there were over 1,000 taxable householders. The town benefitted from the patronage of the York family in the fifteenth century and continued to thrive despite being ransacked after the Rout of Ludford Bridge.

Travelling down Broad Street (the elegant Georgian frontages often cover Tudor interiors), through the Broad Gate (the only one of the medieval gateways into Ludlow still standing, with its thirteenth-century drum towers and portcullis arch) takes you to Ludford Bridge over the river Teme and the small settlement of Ludford, which is older than Ludlow. This route takes you onto the B4361 to Richards Castle and Orleton, roughly the route taken by the Lancastrian forces marching on Ludlow in 1459, though travelling in the other direction.

Ludford Bridge is a three-arch stone bridge built in the fifteenth century. Unfortunately, there is nothing to see to distinguish the site where the opposing armies faced each other and where King Henry VI planted his standard. It is thought that the Yorkist army took up a position just south of Ludford House on the eastern side of the current road. The footpath that loops around the church and the back of the settlement probably goes through the middle of these positions. The king's army halted its march and probably took up position between the current Hucksbarn Farm and the cattle market spanning the current road (in 1459 the lane followed the track that goes behind Hucksbarn). Ludford was separate from Ludlow and was part of the holdings of Richards Castle, and thus the Mortimers of Richards Castle in the thirteenth century. The small church of St Giles is also worth a visit.

Outer Mortimer Tour

A summary of Mortimer connections and remains in each location

The Welsh campaigns of Edward I in 1277 and 1282–3 resulted in the end of native rule in Wales, with the lands divided between the Principality of Wales governed by the Crown, and the Marcher lordships that had emerged during the period of conflict. The 1277 campaign secured the permanent Mortimer control of Maelienydd. Radnor, along with Narberth and parts of Haverford and St Clears, had already been brought into their control by Roger Mortimer's (d.1282) marriage to Maud de Braose. The Marcher lordships of Ceri and Cedewain, with the castle at Dolforwyn, were granted by a grateful king to Roger Mortimer (d.1282) in the years after 1277. Over the next century, further Marcher lordships were acquired through marriage or grant from the Crown. By the late fourteenth century, the Mortimers controlled one-third of the 50 or so Marcher lordships which formed the core of their wealth and power. Although highly controversial at the time, it is not surprising that when he was raised to the rank of earl, Roger Mortimer (d.1330) chose the title 'earl of March'.

23 Clun

Location
In south-west Shropshire, seven miles north of Knighton on the A488.

Mortimer connections
The lordship and castle of Clun were inherited, through marriage, in the twelfth century by the Fitzalan family who already held the lordship of Oswestry and, later, became earls of Arundel and Surrey. In 1231, when John

Clun Castle, from where Maud de Braose defied the sheriff of Shropshire

Fitzalan (d.1240) was wounded in a skirmish (and thought to be dying), the king ordered the castle and lordship to be handed to Ralph Mortimer (d.1246); however, the handover never happened, as a note records that the order was cancelled as Fitzalan still lived. Ralph's granddaughter, Isabel Mortimer, the daughter of Roger Mortimer (d.1282), married Fitzalan's grandson, another John. When Isabel's husband died young in 1267, leaving her with a five-year-old son, custody of Clun was given to her father, Roger Mortimer. In turn, he gave the custody to his wife, Maud de Braose, as various correspondence shows her to be resident there and co-ordinating networks of information about the activities of Llywelyn ap Gruffudd. When Roger Mortimer died in 1282, as usual his lands were seized by the sheriff pending the inquisition to determine their settlement. When the sheriff of Shropshire arrived at Clun, the castle was held by Maud who refused him entrance and shouted insults from the tower. After the sheriff complained to the king, he received a royal command to stop molesting Maud!

The lordship and castle were caught up in the feud that developed in the fourteenth century by later generations of Fitzalans and Mortimers, when the latter opposed the growing domination of the Despensers, the king's favourites. In 1321, Roger Mortimer (d.1330) seized Clun Castle, but this was one castle and lordship that eluded them as control soon reverted to the Fitzalans with whom it remained.

What to see
There are impressive masonry remains of the great keep and some walls within the extensive earthworks of what would have been a magnificent castle. There is free access to the site.

24 MONTGOMERY

Location
In Powys, mid Wales, close to the border with Shropshire, 15 miles north north-west of Clun.

Mortimer connections
The first Montgomery castle was built nearby at Hen Domen in the 1070s by Roger of Montgomery, 1st earl of Shrewsbury. When, 150 years later, Henry III decided in 1223 to build a new castle in stone, he built an almost impregnable stone castle on top of a high ridge one mile to the south-east, with a town founded at its foot. Montgomery remained a royal castle and

The impressive remains of Montgomery Castle (© Paul R. Davis)

lordship for over a century. In November 1276, Roger Mortimer (d.1282) was given command to raise the army to strike into the heart of Wales as part of Edward I's first campaign. Roger, together with the earl of Lincoln, marched out from Montgomery to besiege and capture Llywelyn ap Gruffudd's castle at Dolforwyn. During the period when Roger Mortimer, 1st earl of March (d.1330), was the virtual ruler of the country, he was first granted Montgomery, for a rent of 85 marks, for the period of his life; in 1330, the grant was extended to a hereditary right to himself and his legitimate heirs in perpetuity. It was taken back into royal control after his execution in 1330, however, when his grandson, Roger, the 2nd earl of March (d.1360), succeeded in having the sentence on his grandfather reversed in 1354, he successfully claimed Montgomery as part of his inheritance. The Mortimers' hereditary right to rent Montgomery continued until the death of the 5th earl in 1425, when it passed to Richard, duke of York. When his son, Edward, was crowned, Montgomery reverted fully to the Crown.

What to see

The impressive remains of the large stone castle, with significant amounts of stonework to see, are situated on the crag above the town. There is free access to the site. In the town, St Nicholas' Church contains a fine tomb effigy that has the coat of arms of a younger son of the Mortimer family. It has been claimed that it is the effigy of Sir Edmund Mortimer who held the stewardship

St Nicholas' Church, Montgomery, and the Mortimer effigy

of Montgomery during the minority of his nephew, the 5th earl. Whilst languishing in captivity following his defeat by Owain Glyn Dŵr at Pilleth in 1402, Sir Edmund married Owain's daughter, Katrin, and proclaimed his nephew the rightful king. He died in the siege of Harlech in 1409. The effigy poses an interesting conundrum: the arms on the jupon are those of a younger son of the Mortimers of Wigmore (shown by the differencing in the centre); although repairs were made to the effigy in the nineteenth century, experts date the original work to the early fifteenth century; and as the steward of Montgomery, Sir Edmund was the Mortimer most closely connected to Montgomery in this period. However, given the circumstances of his death as a traitor, it is difficult to see who would have paid for his effigy as doing so would have been seen as traitorous in promoting a Mortimer (and later, Yorkist) claim to the throne. There is also some evidence hinting that Sir Edmund's coat of arms may have been differenced in another way.

25 Dolforwyn Castle

Location
Six miles west south-west of Montgomery, on the west side of the A483.

Mortimer connections
The castle, with a borough at its gates, was first built by Llywelyn ap Gruffudd in 1273 in the cantref of Cedewain. Sited on a hill overlooking the Severn Valley, the location was provocative as it posed a challenge to the royal frontier castle at Montgomery. When Edward I decided on outright war against Llywelyn ap Gruffudd, he launched a three-pronged attack in the north, the south and central Wales. The central army, led by Roger Mortimer (d.1282) and Henry de Lacy, earl of Lincoln, left Montgomery to lay siege to Dolforwyn in 1277, forcing the garrison to surrender. Two years after the defeat of Llywelyn, Roger Mortimer was granted the lordship of Cedewain and Dolforwyn castle. Roger and his descendants repaired and improved the castle, though by the mid fourteenth century it was beginning to decline. The lordship of Cedewain, with Dolforwyn Castle, remained in the ownership of the Mortimers until it passed to the House of York, and thence the Crown.

Aerial view of Dolforwyn Castle, captured by Roger Mortimer (© Crown copyright 2019 CADW)

What to see

In a commanding position on a high ridge above the River Severn, Dolforwyn castle has been the site of one of the most extensive excavations. Forty years ago, only a few fragments of wall could be seen above ground. Painstaking archaeological excavation over 20 years has revealed the extensive ruins that can be seen today. There is free access to the site.

26 Newtown

Location
Four miles south-west of Dolforwyn on the west side of the A483.

Mortimer connections
As soon as he was granted Cedewain with Dolforwyn Castle, Roger Mortimer (d.1282) abandoned Llywelyn's borough outside the castle, replacing it in 1279 with a settlement a short distance away in the Severn Valley in a location much more suited to commerce and trade. A year later, Edward III granted a charter to permit the holding of markets and fairs in the new town.

What to see
There are some remains of Llanfair Chapel linked to St Mary's Church, and a castle tump.

27 CHIRK CASTLE

Location
20 miles north of Oswestry on the west side of the A483/A5.

Mortimer connections
On 2 June 1282, the lands that had belonged to one of the native rulers of northern Powys who had rebelled against Edward I, were granted to Roger Mortimer (d.1326), a younger son of Roger Mortimer of Wigmore (d.1282). The grant of Chirk to a younger son extended the power of the Mortimers into the northern Marches and made Roger Mortimer of Chirk a Marcher lord in his own right. Work to build an imposing new castle at Chirk started in the 1290s, possibly with financial support from Edward I and possibly under the direction of the king's master builder, James of St George. Roger was a powerful baron, being appointed Justiciar of both north and south Wales; however, the rise of the Despenser family, the favourites of Edward II, posed a particular threat to the Mortimers, forcing them into armed opposition. Made to yield to the king, Roger of Chirk was imprisoned in the Tower of London in 1322 with his nephew, Roger Mortimer of Wigmore (d.1330). Although the latter escaped, Roger of Chirk died in the Tower in 1326, shortly before his nephew's triumphant return. While he was imprisoned in the Tower, Chirk was granted to the Fitzalan family; although Roger of Wigmore took possession of Chirk

Chirk Castle, first built by Roger Mortimer of Chirk at the end of the thirteenth century, has been in constant occupation

during his period of power, it reverted to the Fitzalans after his execution in 1330. Although all lands and titles were restored to the Mortimers in 1354, the 2nd earl of March formally released all his rights in the castle of Chirk and the lands of Chirkland to the Fitzalans.

What to see
The magnificent Chirk Castle, now owned by the National Trust, is one of the few buildings (and the only one of the Edwardian castles) to have remained in constant occupation, thus containing buildings, refurbishments and décor that span eight centuries. The north and west curtain walls together with Adam's Tower and the circular Distil Room Tower, which preserve their medieval interiors, remain from the time of Roger Mortimer of Chirk.

28 Denbigh

Location
In Denbighshire in north-east Wales, 26 miles north-west of Wrexham.

Mortimer connections
When Edward I ended native rule in Wales following the campaigns of 1282–83, he created a number of new Marcher lordships, including Denbigh, which he granted to Henry de Lacy, earl of Lincoln and Salisbury (d.1311), one of the commanders of the royal army. Henry de Lacy's immediate priority was to build a castle to secure the district and to provide an administrative centre for the new lordship. The king took a personal interest in the project, spending two weeks in Denbigh planning the new fortifications as well as providing financial support and the services of his master builder, James of St George.

During the period when Roger Mortimer, 1st earl of March (d.1330), was the effective ruler of the country in collaboration with Queen Isabella, he was granted the lordship of Denbigh, thus extending Mortimer influence further into the northern Marcher lordships. After the execution of Roger in 1330, Denbigh was given to William Montagu, later made earl of Salisbury (d.1344), who had been one of the group that captured Roger in Nottingham Castle. However, when the sentence on Roger Mortimer was revoked by Parliament in 1354, his grandson, Roger (d.1360), was able to reclaim all the Mortimer lands and titles, including Denbigh, and become the 2nd earl of March.

Despite repeated petitions to the Crown, the Montagu family failed to reclaim Denbigh; thus, it remained a Mortimer possession, passing to the House of York and then the Crown.

What to see

The impressive castle remains include the remarkable triangular gatehouse formed from three interconnecting octangular towers. The castle is in the care of Cadw and there is an entrance charge. In the town, there are the remains of the medieval town walls, St Hilary's Chapel and Lord Leicester's Church.

RIGHT: The gatehouse of Denbigh Castle, comprising three linked octagonal towers on a triangular plan (reconstruction model © Chris Jones-Jenkins)

BELOW: The castle and town seen from distance, in their landscape context (© Crown copyright 2019 CADW)

29 Builth

Location
Eight miles south of Llandrindod Wells.

Mortimer connections
The lordship of Builth was seized by the de Braose family towards the end of the eleventh century, when Philip de Braose first established a castle. Although at times retaken by the Welsh, it remained in the hands of the de Braose family until 1230. William de Braose (d.1230) had agreed that his daughter would marry Dafydd, the son of Llywelyn ab Iorwerth, with Builth as her dowry. When William was at Llywelyn's court in 1230 to finalise the arrangements for the wedding, he was found in the bedchambers of Llywelyn's wife, Joan. Although William was quickly tried and executed, the marriage between Isobel and Dafydd went ahead, with Llywelyn seizing Builth which he held until his death in 1240.

When Builth was regained by the English after Llywelyn's death, it was taken into the ownership of the Crown. It was granted to the Lord Edward (the heir to the throne) who appointed Roger Mortimer (d.1282) as Constable. Whilst Roger was elsewhere, Llywelyn ap Gruffudd took possession of Builth in 1260, which caused a rift for a time between the royal family and Roger, who was blamed for the loss. Builth was regained by the Crown during Edward I's first campaign of 1277, following which he extensively rebuilt the castle in stone, with a large round keep on top of the motte, surrounded by curtain walls with six towers.

After the forced abdication of Edward II, Builth was given to Queen Isabella for the period of her life, and Roger Mortimer (d.1330) was appointed constable. Shortly after, in 1329 Queen Isabella, with the agreement of Edward III, granted Builth Castle to Roger for a rent of £113 6s 8d per year, payable to her for life. Furthermore, Edward III also granted Roger the reversion of the castle in perpetuity, which had previously been due to the Crown in the event of Queen Isabella's death. The town and castle did revert to the Crown in the circumstances of the execution of Roger Mortimer in 1330 and the queen's loss of position. However, in 1358, Roger Mortimer, the second earl of March (d.1360), recovered it after his own restoration to royal favour. By this time, Builth Castle had been granted to Edward of Woodstock, Prince of Wales (the Black Prince), the heir to the throne, and Roger was required

Aerial view of the mighty earthworks of Builth Castle (© Paul R. Davis)

to pay the rent to him rather than the king. The Mortimer prerogative to rent Builth from the Crown continued as a hereditary right, with successive earls of March renting it from the Black Prince's son, Richard of Bordeaux, and after he became Richard II, from the Crown. The entitlement to rent Builth passed by hereditary right to Richard, duke of York.

What to see
The site of Builth Castle is one of the most striking motte and baileys in Wales and must have been an incredible site when built in stone by Edward I. Nowadays, there is free access to the impressive mound, large embankments, and ditches that remain, though the stonework is long since gone.

30 Elfael: Glan Edw, Colwyn and Painscastle (southern Radnorshire)

Location
Glan Edw Castle and Colwyn Castle are both close to Hundred House, Radnorshire, on the A481, eight miles south-west from Radnor. Glan Edw is on the south side of the A481 (OS 116 543), whilst Colwyn Castle is on the north side (OS 108 540). Painscastle is about seven miles to the south.

Mortimer connections

The cantref of Elfael was seized at the end of the eleventh century, from their base just across the River Wye at Clifford, by the Tosny family who built a castle at Glan Edw in northern Elfael. A castle probably wasn't built in the southern half until the second or third decades of the twelfth century when, with the Tosny family absent in Normandy, the area was administered by Payn fitz John – Painscastle probably taking his name from him. During the twelfth and thirteenth centuries the ownership of Elfael became extremely complicated, with long periods of Welsh rule. In the 1190s, with the Tosny family still absent in Normandy, the de Braose family took the opportunity to seize Elfael, replacing Glan Edw with a new castle at Colwyn. After the execution of William de Braose in 1230, Llywelyn ab Iorwerth went on the offensive in the central March. Henry III launched a counter-attack leading an army into southern Elfael in 1231, where he refurbished the castle at Painscastle, constructing in stone a large royal fortress. One chronicler noted that: 'the king had built one new castle while Llywelyn had destroyed ten.' Shortly after, the king agreed with Llywelyn the division of Elfael, with Llywelyn keeping the northern half. Henry III now granted the southern half to the Tosny family who had finally returned to England.

During the 1240s, Roger Mortimer (d.1282) began to assert his claim to Elfael as the husband of Maud de Braose, one of the heiresses of William de Braose. Although his claims were unsuccessful, in 1257 the Lord Edward granted his royal rights in northern Elfael to Roger Mortimer, the district having been reclaimed by the Crown following the death of Llywelyn in 1240. Three years later, though, Llywelyn ap Gruffudd gained control of northern Elfael in 1260, and Painscastle, in southern Elfael, was surrendered to him by the Treaties of Pipton (1265) and Montgomery (1267). During the campaigns of Edward I in 1277, Roger Mortimer seized Elfael; however, a subsequent royal inquisition decided that the Tosny family were the lawful owners of Painscastle and the southern half, but that Roger, as the heir of the de Braose family, was the rightful owner of Colwyn and the northern half. When Roger Mortimer died in 1282, northern Elfael came under the control of his widow Maud. However, Ralph Tosny had already initiated legal claims to assert his rights to northern Elfael, and eventually the protracted round of legal disputes must have been decided in favour of Tosny, as in 1292 Maud was recorded as holding nothing in Elfael.

What to see

There is no direct access to the sites of Glan Edw and Colwyn, though the motte and baileys can be seen from the local roads. Although Painscastle is also on private land, the owners in the adjacent farm and bungalow are very happy to allow access to the magnificent earthworks which indicate the significant and formidable stone castle that once stood there. The site is also easily visible from the surrounding lanes.

ABOVE: The formidable earthworks of Painscastle still dominate the valley looking west

LEFT: Aerial View of the motte of Glen Edw (© CPAT image 334-001, photograph by Julian Ravest)

31 Clifford

Location
15 miles south-west of Hundred House, near Hay-on-Wye.

Mortimer connections
Clifford Castle was one of the five castles built by William fitz Osbern soon after 1066. When William's son, Roger of Breteuil, forfeited his lands after a failed rebellion in 1075, Clifford was given to the Tosny family. However, the Tosny family were rarely in England, which created the opportunity for Walter fitz Richard fitz Pons to usurp the ownership of Clifford. At first, Walter was the steward of the castle and lordship; then, having married a Tosny daughter, between 1144 and 1154 he began to change his name to Walter Clifford, and usurped the ownership of castle and lordship. Walter's position was consolidated when his daughter, 'The Fair Rosamund' of romantic legend, became the mistress of Henry II. The lordship and castle remained in the possession of the Clifford family until it passed, first to John Giffard, by right of his marriage to Matilda Clifford; then after his death in 1299 it passed to the only child of Matilda's first marriage – Margaret Longespée, who had married Henry de Lacy, earl of Lincoln.

Margaret and Henry's only child, Alice, married Earl Thomas of Lancaster. Following his execution in 1322, Clifford was seized by Hugh Despenser. When he met the same fate in 1326, Clifford reverted to the Crown, until it was granted in 1330 to Roger Mortimer, 1st earl of March (d.1330). Clifford remained in the possession of the Mortimers, descending from them to the House of York and thus the Crown.

Rosamund's Tower

What to see
Clifford Castle is a large site covering four acres to the outermost defences. The castle is in private ownership, though the owners often open it for public visiting annually during the Heritage Open Days in September. It is also easily viewed from nearby lanes, from where the surviving wall structures of the keep and towers, including Rosamund's Tower, can be seen.

Clifford Castle as seen from the other side of the Wye in c.1900
(photograph by Alfred Watkins, courtesy of Hereford Library)

32 Ewyas Lacy and Longtown

Location
South-west Herefordshire between the Golden Valley and the Black Mountains of Wales, 14 miles south of Clifford.

Mortimer connections
Walter de Lacy, who built Ludlow Castle towards the end of the eleventh century, also built a castle at Longtown from where he controlled the whole of the Monnow valley. About 150 years later, another Walter de Lacy died in 1241, leaving two granddaughters to survive him. Ewyas Lacy was split between Maud and Margaret, with the latter holding the castle at Longtown. Margaret married John de Verdun, with the castle and her half of Ewyas Lacy descending in the de Verdun family. Maud married Geoffrey de Geneville, and when their sons also died before them, it was again a granddaughter, Joan de Geneville, who was heir to half of Ewyas Lacy. After Joan married Roger Mortimer (d.1330) in 1301, her share of Ewyas Lacy became the possession of the Mortimers. Although the de Verdun and Mortimer families each owned a half-share (moiety) of, and thus the income from, assets such as the three watermills of Ewyas Lacy, the castle remained in the sole ownership of the de Verdun family. Indeed, in 1359, when Roger Mortimer, 2nd earl of March (d.1360), moved a prisoner from Ewyas Lacy to his castle at Radnor, he had to

The round keep of Longtown Castle, framed by the main entrance archway

petition the king that he held no castle there in which he could securely hold a prisoner. Though the Mortimers never did acquire Longtown Castle, they continued to use the title of lord of Ewyas Lacy, with their share descending to the House of York and then the Crown. Evidence suggests that not owning the castle, and the remoteness from London, disincentivised long-term investment in the district as, by the mid sixteenth century, the Crown's portion was noted to be in complete decay and uninhabitable.

What to see
The castle and village green are surrounded by the massive rampart that was a Roman fort. A small gatehouse, flanked by stone walls, leads from the outer bailey into the inner bailey, in which a circular keep stands on top of a mound. This is one of the earliest round keeps in Britain and the earliest in Wales and the Marcher lordships. It was probably built by Gilbert de Lacy (d. after 1163) who was also the likely builder of the round-naved chapel of St Mary Magdalene in Ludlow Castle.

33 Usk

Location
In Monmouthshire, on the west side of the A449, 15 miles south-west of Monmouth.

Mortimer connections
The first mention of Usk Castle in 1136 shows that it had existed for some time before that as part of the lordship of Chepstow. At the end of the twelfth century, through his marriage to the wealthy heiress, Isabella de Clare, Usk came into the ownership of William Marshal (d.1219), who significantly rebuilt and extended Usk Castle. Although Marshal had five sons, none of them had children, thus each inherited successively. On the death of the last son, Anselm in 1245, Usk became a separate lordship inherited by his nephew Richard de Clare, earl of Gloucester and Hereford, whose grandson, Gilbert, was killed at Bannockburn in 1314. On Gilbert's death, Usk and some of the Clare lands in east England passed to one of his co-heirs, his sister Elizabeth, the widow of John de Burgh, earl of Ulster. Though Elizabeth de Burgh (née de Clare, d.1360) had two further husbands, her inheritance passed through her son by John de Burgh, William Dom de Burgh, 3rd earl of Ulster (who died, murdered in 1333, 27 years before his mother), to her granddaughter, Elizabeth de Burgh, 4th countess of Ulster (d.1363). Elizabeth married Lionel, duke of Clarence, the second surviving son of Edward III. Their only child, Philippa, 5th countess of Ulster, married Edmund Mortimer, 3rd earl of March (d.1381), in 1368. Thus, Usk, along with the other Clare lands inherited by Philippa's great-grandmother, passed to the Mortimers. Philippa also brought to the Mortimers the earldom of Ulster and, as the granddaughter of Edward III, her children by Edmund Mortimer came into the line of succession to the throne.

Edmund and Philippa must have resided at Usk as their eldest son, Roger (4th earl of March, d.1398), was born in the castle. The Mortimers established an important first charter for the town of Usk and were possibly responsible for building the round Dovecote Tower and Gatehouse in the outer curtain wall. The family became early patrons of the chronicler, Adam of Usk, who was born in the castle gatehouse. After the death of Edmund Mortimer, 5th earl of March, in 1425, Usk passed to his nephew and heir, Richard, duke of York (d.1360), thus becoming a property of the Crown when Richard's son was crowned Edward IV.

What to see

The extensive ruins of the castle stand above the charming medieval market town of Usk. The Mortimers were possibly responsible for building the outer gatehouse and the round 'Dovecote Tower' in the outer wall. The castle is privately owned but is open to visitors on certain days for a small charge.

LEFT: The Great Keep at Usk Castle (© Paul R. Davis); RIGHT: The Garrison Tower

34A NARBERTH AND 34B ST CLEARS

Location
Narberth is to the south of the A40, 21 miles west of Carmarthen; St Clears is 12 miles east of Narberth on the A40.

Mortimer connections
NARBERTH
The early history of the lordship of Narberth was bound up in the Norman incursions by the Montgomery family, earls of Shrewsbury, into south-west Wales in 1093, when Pembroke Castle was first built. Although the first written record of a castle at Narberth is in 1116, it is unclear who held the lordship for periods during the twelfth century. By the early thirteenth century, Narberth was probably part of the lands of the earl of Pembroke,

The remains of Narberth Castle

William Marshal (d.1219), descending to each of his five sons as each, in turn, died childless. When the fifth son, Anselm, died childless in 1245, the great estates of William Marshal were divided between his daughters and granddaughters. Narberth passed to his daughter Eva, the wife of William de Braose who had been executed by Llywelyn ab Iorwerth in 1230. Eva and William had four daughters, who became the co-heirs of the great de Braose inheritance as well as Eva's share of the Marshal inheritance. One of those daughters, Maud de Braose (d.1301) inherited the lordships of Narberth and Radnor, plus one-third shares of Haverford and St Clears, and when she married Roger Mortimer (d.1282) Narberth passed into the ownership of the Mortimer family.

Not long after, a Welsh invasion in 1257 destroyed the castle, with many of the garrison slain. Following this, Roger Mortimer rebuilt Narberth Castle in stone. After Roger's death in 1282, Maud de Braose granted the lordship of Narberth to a younger son, Roger Mortimer of Chirk (d.1326).

ST CLEARS

The early history of the lordship and castle of St Clears is very unclear. It was possibly first founded by a family that participated in the sea-borne incursions into south-west Wales in the 1090s. After it was captured by Welsh forces in 1189, it was recaptured by William de Braose (d.1211) who now claimed ownership; however, when he fell out with King John, it was taken into royal hands, only to be captured again by the Welsh. When it was regained by the English, William's son, Reginald (d.1228), was allowed to inherit, having made

Aerial view of the site of St Clears Castle, with the motte top-left (© Paul R. Davis)

his peace with the new regime of the infant Henry III. When Reginald's son, William, was executed by Llywelyn ab Iorwerth in 1230, the de Braose lands were inherited by his daughters, with one-third of St Clears going to each of Eva, Maud and Eleanor. As they were minors at the time of their father's death, their lands were held in wardship. As each daughter married, respectively Cantilupe, Mortimer and de Bohun, their one-third shares of St Clears merged with the estates of their husbands, Maud's husband being Roger Mortimer (d.1282).

Maud gave her one-third part of St Clears to her younger son, Roger Mortimer of Chirk, at the same time that she gave him the lordship of Narberth. As his one-third portion of St Clears bordered his lordship of Narberth, it was now subsumed into that lordship.

NARBERTH AND THE MORTIMER PORTION OF ST CLEARS

Roger of Chirk was imprisoned in the Tower of London in 1322 following the failed rebellion against the Despensers and Edward II, and the king made Rhys ap Gruffydd keeper of the lordship of Narberth, including St Clears, for the period of his lifetime. Although his nephew, Roger Mortimer of Wigmore (d.1330), escaped from the Tower, Roger of Chirk died there in 1326 shortly before his nephew's triumphant return. Despite the claims of the surviving son of Roger of Chirk, Roger Mortimer claimed Narberth for himself during the period of his de-facto rule of the country. His execution in 1330 triggered various claims and counterclaims for ownership of Narberth. The outcome was that Edward III restored Narberth, with the portion of St Clears, to Rhys ap Gruffydd who seems to have held it until Roger Mortimer (d.1360) obtained the reversal of the judgement on his father, becoming the 2nd earl of March. However, he was able to recover Narberth from Rhys only after the courts ruled in his favour in June 1354.

When the 2nd earl died in 1360, Narberth, with their portion of St Clears, became part of the dower of his widow, Philippa, who held it until her death in 1382. The Mortimers retained Narberth and their one-third share of St Clears until the death of Edmund Mortimer, 5th earl of March in 1425, when it passed to his heir, Richard, duke of York.

What to see
There is free access to the remains of the stone castle at Narberth that was built by Roger Mortimer (d.1282).

The earthen remains of a castle at St Clears are now part of a park at the south end of the town. All that is visible is the large earthen motte that stands at the northern end of what was a large bailey.

35 Haverford (Haverfordwest)

Location
11 miles west of Narberth on the A40.

Mortimer connections
The Marcher lordship of Haverford was established during the royally sponsored Flemish immigration into the area in the early 1100s, when the castle was built by Tancred. For reasons unknown, his grandson was deprived of all his lands by King John in 1210, who subsequently granted Haverford to William Marshal, earl of Pembroke (d.1219). Marshal and his sons granted a charter to Haverford and other benefits that enabled it to become a successful commercial and trading centre. When Anselm Marshal died childless in 1245, Haverford was inherited by Eva, one of the daughters of William Marshal (d.1219). On her death, Haverford was divided between her three surviving daughters by William de Braose (d.1330), Eva, Maud and Eleanor, with each

third passing into the families of their husbands, respectively Cantilupe, Mortimer and de Bohun. Shortly after the partition, William Cantilupe gave his third share to Humphrey de Bohun (d.1265), the husband of Eleanor. Owning two-thirds of Haverford, the de Bohuns were the major players in the lordship; however, in 1289 they exchanged their two-thirds with Queen Eleanor, the wife of Edward I, who had fallen in love with the town. After her death, her portion remained in the hands of the Crown until granted to Aymer de Valence, earl of Pembroke in 1307. When he died childless in 1324, it reverted again to the Crown.

Throughout this time the Mortimer third had been less significant; however, when Maud de Braose granted Narberth to her younger son, Roger of Chirk (d.1286), she also granted him her third share of Haverford. Although Roger of Chirk died in the Tower of London in 1326, his nephew, Roger Mortimer of Wigmore (d.1330) became the de-facto ruler of England following the forced abdication of Edward II. During the period of his ascendancy, the 1st earl of March took all of Haverford for himself, then granted the whole to Queen Isabella, who kept it till her death, when it passed to her grandson, the Black Prince, the eldest son of Edward III. After the death of the Black Prince, it passed to his son, Richard, and on his coronation, it thus merged with the Crown.

What to see

The remains of the castle, in the town now called Haverfordwest, originate from the works carried out by Queen Eleanor of Castile, the wife of Edward I, who fell in love with Haverford and acquired it for herself in 1289. The Augustinian Priory was built downstream of Haverford Castle in the time of the Fleming Robert fitz Richard (d.1211). The current priory site features a restored medieval garden that was uncovered during excavations in the 1980s. It is the only surviving ecclesiastical medieval garden in Britain.

Haverford Castle (© Paul R. Davis)

OTHER MORTIMER PLACES TO VISIT NEAR TO THE WELSH MARCHES

NB All geographical directions are from Wigmore

NORTH-EAST
Chelmarsh

Mortimer connections
By the early twelfth century, Chelmarsh was part of the possessions of the Mortimer family. Around 1150, Hugh Mortimer (d.1181–85) gave the revenues from Chelmarsh church to the house of Augustinian canons, which later became Wigmore Abbey. Throughout the later twelfth and the thirteenth centuries, Chelmarsh was granted to one of the younger Mortimer sons; however, around 1250 it became the permanent possession of a younger son of Ralph Mortimer (d.1246), Hugh, and it remained in the possession of his heirs until the early fifteenth century – the Mortimers of Chelmarsh.

What to see
The village is dominated by St Peter's Church, much of which dates from the Mortimer period.

Bridgnorth

Mortimer connections
The royal castle of Brug came into the control of Hugh Mortimer (d.1181–85) during the Anarchy in the reign of King Stephen. When Henry I required all the former royal castles to be surrendered to the Crown, Hugh refused. The king besieged Bridgnorth, Cleobury and Wigmore. When Cleobury and Wigmore fell, Hugh submitted and gave up Bridgnorth but was not punished further.

During the Despenser wars of the early 1320s, the forces of Roger Mortimer (d.1330) and his uncle, Roger Mortimer of Chirk, were desperately trying to prevent the royal army from crossing the River Severn. When a royal vanguard secured the bridge at Bridgnorth in January 1322, Roger and his uncle attacked and defeated the royal force, with the bridge and much of the town burned. The conflict moved up river to Shrewsbury where Roger and his uncle were forced to submit.

What to see
The remains of Bridgnorth Castle are set on a cliff by the side of the River Severn. Today the castle is little more than a ruin, comprising of a 70-foot-tall, twelfth-century Norman tower and some other insubstantial stonework built in the time of Henry II. The tower leans at an alarming angle of 15 degrees, three times greater than that of the leaning tower of Pisa. This is due to an attempt to blow it up during the Civil War.

EAST
Ashford Carbonel

Mortimer connections
The manor of Ashford Carbonel belonged to the lords of Richards Castle and thus the Mortimers of Richards Castle during the thirteenth century.

What to see
The Church of St Mary retains a number of features from the period of the Mortimers of Richards Castle, and earlier.

Cleobury Mortimer

Mortimer connections
Cleobury was a long-standing Mortimer lordship. It was one of the manors owned by Queen Edith, the widow of Edward the Confessor, which was given to Ralph Mortimer (d.1115–27) after she died in 1075. During the twelfth and thirteenth centuries it was the centre of the Mortimer estates in Shropshire and was a favoured residence of Hugh (d.1181–85) and his son Roger (d.1214), one of whose sons was buried in the church. The Mortimers retained ownership throughout their long history. In 1155, when Hugh refused to surrender Bridgnorth to the new king, Henry II besieged not only Bridgnorth but also Cleobury and Wigmore. Cleobury castle was destroyed, though it was subsequently rebuilt on a different site near the church. At a great age Hugh 'retired' to and died at Cleobury between 1181–85. In the 1260s Roger (d.1282) manipulated certain privileges to create the powers of a Marcher lord in Cleobury and his surrounding estates in Shropshire.

What to see
The Church of St Mary dates from *c*.1160 with rebuilding and extensions during the fourteenth and fifteenth centuries. The St Nicholas Chapel was founded by either the first or second earl of March and is mentioned in 1359. The church was restored in 1874–75 by Sir George Gilbert Scott and its prominent features are the leaning walls and the twisted spire which forms a distinctive local landmark.

In a commanding position to the east of the town is a site now known as Castle Toot (from the old English 'tote' meaning 'lookout hill'). This was probably a motte and bailey castle, besieged and destroyed by the forces of Henry II. There are no remains, and a large house now occupies the site. The castle was rebuilt on a new site by the church, of which only traces of the moat remain. This is where Hugh (d.1181–85) lived out his last years, and was an important administrative centre for the Mortimer estates in Shropshire.

Kinlet

Mortimer connections
Kinlet was an early Mortimer church held by their subtenants. It was granted to Wigmore Abbey by John Brampton towards the end of the twelfth century. The Mortimers, passionate about hunting, developed a deer park on part of the nearby estate of Earnwood for their private use; this was never let out to tenants, eventually being absorbed into the Crown property when Edward IV became king.

What to see
The church of St John the Baptist is a fine building with much of it constructed in the early thirteenth century and the early fourteenth century. The tower was probably added in the thirteenth century and the two pillars under its arch sport several carved heads which may represent members of the Mortimer or Brampton families.

Martley

Mortimer connections
Although a Mortimer Chapel has existed in the church since the early fourteenth century, it is not clear what the Mortimer connection was in that period. Later in the fourteenth century a descendant of Roger Mortimer of Chirk became lord of Martley through marriage and they held Martley during the fifteenth century.

What to see
The church of St Peter contains a fine alabaster effigy of a late fifteenth-century knight. It may represent Hugh Mortimer, who died in 1460, a descendant of Roger of Chirk. It has often been said that Hugh was killed at the battle of Wakefield; however, the inquisition post mortem shows that he had in fact died six months or so before the battle. The effigy depicts him in a suit of plate armour with escalloped taces, from which are suspended tuilles.

Warwick

Mortimer connections
Catherine Mortimer (d.1369), daughter of Roger (d.1330) and Joan de Geneville and born in Ludlow, married Thomas Beauchamp, earl of Warwick.

What to see
The splendid medieval church of St Mary contains the magnificent effigy of Catherine Mortimer and her husband, Thomas. The figures around the tomb give a rich picture of medieval dress, and Mortimer Arms are embossed on the ceiling.

Kenilworth

Mortimer connections
Kenilworth was Simon de Montfort's stronghold besieged by Prince Edward and Roger Mortimer (d.1282) after the Battle of Evesham 1265. In 1279 Roger held a great tournament with over 100 knights at Kenilworth Castle, which he was holding in the absence of the earl of Lancaster, to celebrate the knighthoods of his three sons. The tournament was a

'Round Table' with Arthurian associations. It was also where Edward II was first held following his fall at the hands of Roger Mortimer and Queen Isabella, and where he was persuaded to renounce the throne in favour of his son.

What to see
Kenilworth Castle is owned by English Heritage and there is a charge for entry. The significant remains include the imposing twelfth-century keep, and John of Gaunt's Great Hall. The gatehouse guarding the entrance from the causeway to the outer court of the castle, is called Mortimer's Tower, possibly named after Roger.

SOUTH-EAST
Much Marcle

Mortimer connections
During the thirteenth century the Mortimers acquired an interest in the manor of Much Marcle. The church stands next to the old castle mound known as Mortimer's Castle. Within the large church are several tombs, three of which may be to members of the Mortimer family.

What to see
St Bartholomew's Church is famous for the outstanding restored tomb of Blanche Mortimer (d.1347), daughter of Roger Mortimer, 1st earl of March (d.1330) and wife of Sir Peter Grandison, 2nd Baron Grandison (d.1358). In October 2013 restorers were surprised to discover Blanche's coffin inside the monument itself, rather than in the ground beneath. Blanche's body had been wrapped in what almost looked like a lead shroud. There are many Mortimer shields on the tomb. There is also an unusual wooden painted effigy of Walter de Helyon, a Mortimer and Grandison steward.

The motte and bailey castle is just to the north of the church. There is no public access to the site though the 30m-high motte can be seen from the churchyard through the cottages that have been built in the bailey. The stone from the castle ruins was used to build the church tower.

Fladbury

Mortimer connections
The 'Mortimer' interest in the church centres on a window with fourteenth-century glass showing six coats of arms. These are all clearly related to the Battle of Evesham in 1265. It is said that the glass was transferred from Evesham Abbey following the Dissolution.

What to see
The stained glass window of St John the Baptist, Fladbury shows the coats of arms of Roger Mortimer (d.1282) and Simon de Montfort and four others connected with the Battle of Evesham, including Hugh Despenser, whose death at Evesham started the feud with the Mortimers that came to a head in the 1320s with the deposition of Edward II.

Evesham

Mortimer connections
The Battle of Evesham on 4 August 1265 was the violent and blood-soaked conclusion of the Barons' Rebellion led by Simon de Montfort (see p. 29). Although he had initially been inclined to support the rebellion, Roger Mortimer (d.1282) had become a key supporter of the king. During the years before 1265 the feud between Mortimer and de Montfort had become more intense, with each side resorting to violence, including the siege of Wigmore Castle. Roger was a key commander of the royal army at Evesham and according to one source personally killed Simon de Montfort. After the battle, Simon's head was struck off and transported to Wigmore Castle as a grisly trophy for Roger's wife, Maud de Braose.

What to see
Simon de Montfort was buried under the altar of Evesham Abbey, which was subsequently destroyed at the Dissolution of the Monasteries in the sixteenth century. Only the magnificent Abbey Bell Tower remains. In 1965 a memorial of stone from Montfort-l'Amaury in France was laid on the site of the former altar in Evesham Abbey Park Gardens. The fourteenth-century Almonry is a fascinating heritage centre which has a permanent display about Simon de Montfort. There is a self-guided Simon de Montfort battle-trail walk with information boards around the site of the battle.

SOUTH
Berkeley Castle

Mortimer connections
This is the castle where Edward II was imprisoned after his deposition as king. It was reported in 1327 that he had died whilst at Berkeley Castle and a body was buried at Gloucester Cathedral. Rumours circulated that he had been killed on the instructions of Roger Mortimer (d.1330), who had been instrumental in his downfall, and it was one of the crimes that Roger was convicted of and executed for in 1330. However (and as discussed on p. 43), there is evidence, hotly disputed, that Edward II did not die at Berkeley and survived for a number of years.

What to see
The castle has been owned and lived in by the same family for 850 years. There is an admission charge to visit the extensive remains, including the King's Gallery with the cell and dungeon in which Edward II was imprisoned.

Bristol Cathedral

Mortimer connections and what to see
In the Elder Lady Chapel there is a fine tomb of Lady Margaret Mortimer 1304–37, and her son Maurice, Lord Berkeley. She was a daughter of Roger Mortimer (d.1330) and Joan de Geneville, and had married Thomas de Berkeley in 1320.

FURTHER READING

ON THE MORTIMERS

Hopkinson, Charles and Speight, Martin, *The Mortimers: Lords of the March* (Logaston Press, 2002, reprinted 2011)

Mortimer, Ian, *The Greatest Traitor: The Life of Sir Roger Mortimer, Ruler of England 1327–1330* (Vintage Books, 2003)

ON THE HISTORY AND DEVELOPMENT OF THE WELSH MARCHES

Davies, R.R., *The Age of Conquest: Wales 1063–1415* (Oxford University Press, 1987, reprinted 2006)

—, *Lordship and Society in the March of Wales 1282–1400* (Oxford University Press, 1978, reprinted 2005)

Davis, Paul R., *The Forgotten Castles of Wales and the Marches* (Logaston Press, revised edition 2022)

Fleming, John, *The Welsh Marcher Lordships II: South-West* (Logaston Press, due 2023)

Hodges, Geoffrey, *Owain Glyn Dŵr & the War of Independence in the Welsh Borders* (Logaston Press, 1995)

Hume, Philip, *The Welsh Marcher Lordships I: Central & North* (Logaston Press, 2021)

Lieberman, Max, *The Medieval March of Wales: The Creation and Perception of a Frontier, 1066–1283* (Cambridge University Press, paperback edition 2013)

Remfry, Paul, *Castles of Radnorshire* (Logaston Press, 1996)

Rowley, Trevor, *The Welsh Border: Archaeology, History and Landscape* (Tempus, revised edition 2001)

Stephenson, David, *Medieval Wales c.1050–1332: Centuries of Ambiguity* (University of Wales Press, 2019)

ON THE GENERAL HISTORY OF THE MEDIEVAL PERIOD

Carpenter, David, *The Struggle for Mastery, The Penguin History of Britain 1066–1284* (Penguin Books, 2004)

Jones, Dan, *The Plantagenets: The Kings who made England* (Collins, 2013)

Mortimer, Ian, *The Time Traveller's Guide to Medieval England* (Vintage, 2009)
Rubin, Miri, *The Hollow Crown, A History of Britain in the Late Middle Ages* (Penguin Books, 2006)
Warner, Kathryn, *Edward II: The Unconventional King* (Amberley, 2014)

On local matters

Brookes, Alan and Pevsner, Nikolaus, *The Buildings of England – Herefordshire* (Yale University Press, 2012)
Burtscher, Michael, *The Fitzalans, Earls of Arundel and Surrey, Lords of the Welsh Marches, 1267–1415* (Logaston Press, 2008)
Caird, R., Cherry, J., Hume, P. & Wood, H., *The Ludlow Castle Heraldic Roll* (Logaston Press, 2019)
Cook, Martin & Kidd, Neil, *The March of Ewyas: The Story of Longtown Castle and the de Lacy Dynasty* (Logaston Press, 2020)
Griffiths, Ralph A., Hopkins, Tony, and Howell, Ray (eds), *The Gwent County History Vol 2: The Age of the Marcher Lords, c.1070–1536* (University of Wales Press, 2008)
Hodges, Geoffrey, *Ludford Bridge and Mortimers Cross* (Logaston Press, 2014)
Johnson, Andy and Karen, *Walking the Old Ways of Herefordshire* (Logaston Press, revised edition 2022)
Johnson, Andy and Karen, *Walking the Old Ways of Radnorshire* (Logaston Press, 2016)
Johnson, Andy and Karen, *Walking the Old Ways of South Shropshire* (Logaston Press, 2019)
Johnson, Andy and Karen, *Walking the Old Ways of East Breconshire and the Black Mountains* (Logaston Press, 2022)
Knight, Jeremy K. & Johnson, Andy (eds), *Usk Castle, Priory and Town* (Logaston Press, 2008)
Roberts, Graham, *Around and About Herefordshire and the Southern Welsh Marches* (Logaston Press, 2004)
Scourfield, Robert and Haslam, Richard, *The Buildings of Wales – Powys* (Yale University Press, 2013)
Shoesmith, Ron and Johnson, Andy (eds), *Ludlow Castle: Its History and Buildings* (Logaston Press, 2006)
Thurlby, Malcolm, *The Herefordshire School of Romanesque Sculpture* (with a history of the Anarchy in Herefordshire by Bruce Coplestone-Crow) (Logaston Press, 2013)
Walker R.F., *Pembrokeshire County History, Vol II: Medieval Pembrokeshire* (Pembrokeshire Historical Society, 2002)